I0831020

Copyright ©2021 by Concep3D

International Cataloging Data in the Publication (ICDP)

<table><tr><td>

C972.d   Cunico, Marlon Wesley Machado,

The Agile Creativity: Be more productive, innovative and creative / Marlon Wesley Machado Cunico; Concep3D Pesquisas Científicas Ltda; Curitiba, 2021,

ISBN: 9798518974715

1.Innovation; 2. creativity 3. Technology.   Título

CDD 620
</td></tr></table>

Systematic Cataloging Index

1. Engineering and applications 620

1st Edition - 2021

Printed in Brazil

©2021 by Concep3D, All Rights Reserved

Concep3D Pesquisas Científicas Ltda

298 Pedro Ivo street ap 23

80010-020 Curitiba, Brasil

http://www.concep3d.com

THE AGILE CREATIVITY

Be more productive, innovative and creative

Responsibility Term

All the strategies and information that you will read in this book, and what I learned when I started in engineering and businesses development to increase the value of my products are fruit of my professional experiences in the area, in addition to more than 15 years of scientific research in Product Development, Problem Solving and Additive and advanced manufacturing.

Although I did my best to ensure the accuracy and the highest quality of this information, in way that all the techniques and methods taught here are highly effective for anyone who is not inclined to learn and put the suitable effort required to apply them as instructed, these methods and information is not possible to be learned theoretically, but only in the practice.

The strategies and information presented here are for all, but not for anyone. You need to be willing. In addition, your particular situation may not be adequate perfectly to the methods and techniques taught in this guide. So, you can use it by adjusting the information according to your specific need and, for that reason, results may vary from person to person. There is no guarantee, there is only one experience and testimony of thousands of customers successful thanks to this method.

My name is Marlon Cunico, I born in Londrina (Brazil) in 1984. My parents moved to Curitiba (Parana Capitol) looking for a better life.

Both of my parents came from humble family, where only my mother had come to University. As a consequence, life was hard and unfair several times .

My father is a wise man who graduated in Mathematics and Physics, even though he had to work in 2 or 3 different jobs to support our family. In addition, my mother used to work 60 hours per week in order to pay my studies.

I studied as hard as it was possible because we could not afford to pay private College. Therefore, I was accepted in one of the most prestigious Engineering University in Brazil on year before I finish high school.

After 7 years , I finished Engineering, Mastering in Engineering and Material Sciences and got my Ph.D. in Robotics and Advanced Manufacturing.

In 2011, I was working in the department of innovation and engineering of one of the biggest automotive Industries in the globe.

Years before, I had started working with Rapid prototyping technologies (which become 3D printing after some time). I was so fascinated about such amazing technologies that **I invented and patented a brand new process by the end of my Mastering thesis**. I had realized that these technologies would change the world as we had known. They changed indeed, and 9 years after that moment, several researchers and experts indicate that 3D printers boost the 4th industrial revolution.

Therefore, I took one of the most difficult decisions of my life. I founded my first company. The main goal of that company was to produce prototypes and low scale production batches applying 3D printing technologies.

Amazing, isn't it? That is right.

But in 2013, the biggest popularization of 3D printing technologies happened and thousand of 3D printing enthusiasts have got exactly the same conclusion that I had before.

We started playing the game using the tools that big companies (majorly manufactures of 3D printing) sold to us. We optimized 3D printing parameters, used and developed closed chambers and achieved 3D printing results that were unbelievable.

Things looked like a roller-coaster. Part of clients that understood foundations of 3D printing were ok with our deliveries. But major of clients who did not give a damn about 3D printing techniques and their parameters were extremely unhappy with results that in general way were outstanding.

I saw around 82% of companies from that time closing their doors and then I decided to dedicate my research career to innovation and advanced manufacturing.

I realized that everyone was playing with wrong rules which were defined by big corporations that just wanted to sell you their machines. The tools that were provided were obsolete and aim to validate the advantages of their equipments against the competitors.

Then, I start developing a guideline which maps customers need and ensures suitable resu ts for my clients. This was the moment when the **table start turning over** .

I was professor and researcher at University in addition to managing company. Then **I launched new research** which aimed to investigate the contribution of **creativity techniques in product development and innovation** of several segments altogether.

We identify that the product launching of most of businesses and companies which did not use neither creativity methods nor systematic product failed. Similarly, this research also indicated that people that did not apply innovation / creativity techniques at work were less successful than people who applied such amazing techniques.

The conclusion was obvious thus, start applying creativity techniques. But the reality was harder than the key indicators of paper. Corporations and people do not want to be changed and **severe changes needed to be implemented** in order to achieve such amazing results.

We started to collect, modify and develop different techniques upon Lean manufacturing, Toyota techniques, Six Sigma, Open source technologies, Jewelry, foundry and casting among others.

As a result, my company survived to the storm, increased profits in 50 times and obtained more than $500k in funds and projects per year.

After solving the most dangerous threat of our company. I have been seeing the same problem happen over and over again, killing thousands of companies nowadays. Therefore **I decided to share and teach other people and entrepreneurs** about what I worked for me.

In several events people were learned how to change their mind and improve their services to another level.

Now, my goal is to bring this message to as many people as possible. And for that reason I am sharing the essence of the best practices in this book.

BE BOLD, MAKE IT HAPPEN !!!!!!!!!!!

Your learning and self development is directly proportional to the energy, focus and immersion in the subjects you want to learn. It is not just a valid observation for advanced manufacturing and finishing techniques, it is also true for everything that you intend to learn.

So, one of the things you will need to do is to create your "own world", where in much of the time you will practically breathe creativity and innovation.

This book will be your central guide, but read a good part of it and spend the rest of your day watching TV is not going to help quite much. You'll need more control about the inputs information you are handling, especially when you finish this book and start applying strategies in your business.

So I would like to share with you some tips to facilitate your immersion process in that brand new innovative universe:

1. A step further

Take time to become an overachiever! Watch the complementary videos I prepared for you expand your knowledge. In them, I count the my story and what brought me here, comment excerpts from the book, I give examples and much more!

2. Take notes

Try to read calmly and summarize the main contents in a notebook. Do it in such a way that you can explain the content learned to another person.

3. Subscribe to my YouTube channel

https://www.youtube.com/channel/UC8QFph7-R2YERpN5cEAl1Mw

There, you will find great views of the world of advanced manufacturing.

4. Follow my Instagram profile

https://www.instagram.com/concep3D

Daily pills of wisdom and backstage of everyday life an entrepreneur.

5. Subscribe to my newsletter

For you who are a fan of audio content, look for Marlon Cunico in his favorite podcast application.

6. Create study group

Refer this book to others and form a group of studies. Discuss the book's content with friends, colleagues and close people helps you to go beyond. Remember: if you want to go fast, go alone, otherwise if you want to go far, go accompanied.

"Minds are like parachutes; they work best when open."

Thomas Dewar

Summary

I believe that this book is going to be very useful for quite many people. On the one hand, it is extraordinary for those who have already innovation and creativity.

In addition, the strategies that I expose here go further and helps to create an infinity of new sort of businesses, processes innovation and productivity. Therefore, I have several case studies in different segments, such as health care, medical application, industry, games, dentistry, product design, maintenance, services, robotics, engineering, architecture and many others.

I will be very glad if you finish this book and realize the multiple opportunities and potential application of those methodologies.

During this book, I will also presents a creativity strategy which several companies, such as Google and Squarespace, adopted and that I implemented in my company in order to make it rise. This strategy is so unbelievable that it allowed me to:

- Have the highest profit margin which I have ever seen in the planet
- Have a lean structure, with few employees (where I was not even physically present most of the time)

- Kickoff with an investment which is so small that everyone could implement
- Make your clients extremely happy and faithful
- Have outstanding results

You will discover this strategy along this book. But first, I will have to teach you 2 very important things in order you to understand why this strategy is so worthy.

1. What creativity and innovation bring to you and your company

You will learn to use, in your business or personal designs, a creativity and innovation strategies that will bring **measurable and quantitative results**.

Measuring each action and project that you deliver will allow you to **scale your results and investments in a super reduced risk environment** . Therefore, it will help your business to improve in addition to create new branches and new opportunities.

The best part is that **you don't need to begin with a millionaire budget**. Invest wisely a very small budget is enough to improve your projects and increase results.

One thing I can ensure to you, after finishing this part of book, you are never going to see the innovation and creativity from the same point of view. For 99%

companies and businesses wrongly believe that innovation is a big black box where the most impressive high technologies will provide them competitiveness .

After finishing this part of book, you will be part of 1% of people who understand what happens inside the mysterious black box.

After explaining that to you, I will teach you:

2. How to create and take advantage of a productive and creative environment

In this part of the book, I will explain to you **how to create and take advantage of a productive and creative environment** in a step-by-step guidance. This strategy unbelievably works for those who either have experience or are beginning from zero point.

Do you want to know why this strategy is so extraordinary? Because it allows you to:

- Optimize your job time
- Deliver an accurate, precise and high quality product or service
- Handle multiple project simultaneously
- Increase your value in accordance with your client satisfaction

- Create metrics to always reach the peak performance from the customer point of view
- Increase your profits – a lot

Well, do you know why I organized this book in this fashion way? Because although you haven't implemented creativity nor innovative methods in your environment, the best thing you can do now is to learning about the strategies that actually work.

Imagine one thing, If you don't know how to create innovative solutions for problems and I am just giving you the magic strategy on a silver plate; This terrific method will make absolutely no sense for you and you won't be able to move from wherever you are.

On the other hand, what I show in this book is so powerful that, I am sure, it will be almost impossible to ignore this new projects and design, even if you already have yours.

I have countless case studies of people who created new business units or pivoted your business to this new strategy, after find out what I'm going to teach you.

I truly believe that the content of this book can transform your way to work, design and solve problems. I say so because this content transform my company and thousands of peoples whom I mentored during the years.

Therefore, **it is very important you consume the contents of this book in the sequence in which it is presented to you**.

 Believe in me, I have spend quite many hours in order to find the best way to present the worldwide best practices which is presented to you so you can **consume, learn and apply as efficiently as possible**.

And, moreover: **read, learn, apply and tell people around you!**

1

Part 1 - What creativity and innovation bring to you and your company

1 How are extraordinary results possible to be reached?

The results obtained by people who learned the best practices that you will learn in this book are extraordinary! Best of all, I honestly believe that anyone that is really committed to learn and apply the strategies proposed in this book will reach good rewards.

I do not identify it by intuition, but according to over 2000 case studies which I cataloged from scientists, engineers, designer, businesses which partially implemented tools and strategies that I teach you in this book.

"Minds are like parachutes; they work best when open."

Thomas Dewar

As a consequence, many of them reported increase of value over 20 times besides obtaining leadership of specific business segments. That is an extraordinary result.

Nonetheless, don't mess results up. Results like this in the first campaign is abnormal. The proposed strategy tend to be more like a transformation of company philosophy. In this case, let's call it **Innovation Transformation**.

What do I mean by that?

I mean that not everyone will reach this sort of result.

Do you know why?

Because although it is possible, to do what you have to do to achieve such results is not easy. In this book I'm going to give the map and point the direction

Nevertheless, the effort and dedication to study, learn and apply the tools depends entirely on you.

 As the old proverb says : "**You can lead a horse to water, but you can't make it drink** ".

And unfortunately, not everyone has the willing to do their part, to enter the field and not to give up on first stumbling block or obstacle.

Reading this book and continuing to be seated in the chair, doing nothing, will not make the results appear magically for you.

But if you have enough will to both roll up your sleeves and go to the combat, this book will give you the path that many have already taken to get there.

So, now that all the cards are on the table, how is it possible to have extraordinary results?

2 To innovate, or not to innovate ? That is the question.

First of all, you will have to understand that there are 3 type of innovative opportunities that you can apply creativity and innovation development techniques. The comprehension of these opportunities will allow you to create suitable strategies to better achieve the goal. Therefore, it is possible to reach peak of efficiency for most or all clients in accordance with your strategy flexibility. Eventually, this strategy will put you in the stage as main star of a segment.

Types of Opportunities

Let's imagine that all the opportunities are like an Iceberg. Most of times, only the tip of iceberg is visible (out of water) . In this case, the iceberg tip illustrate our first type of opportunity. Nonetheless, this opportunity is the most developed by the competition , which intends to create instantaneous effect on the customers.

Well, you must have been imaging which type of opportunity is this?

The SII have 3 main benefits:

- It is fast to be implemented and developed
- It does not required extensive methods of creativity or Innovation.
- It will help you to bring attention to your products, work or services

In this type of opportunity, you have to put almost no efforts to implement and convince people about their benefits. Normally, you don't even need to develop it because it appears naturally from the experience in some field/segment.

As a consequence, your products gain value and catch attention of your customers in addition to changing almost nothing in the organization philosophy nor the product, service or processes.

That is why most of companies/workers kill themselves for the tip of iceberg. Therefore, that is exactly where your main competitors are working hard to steal your clients. Thus, it will lead you to compete in a price, reducing your profit margin and jeopardizing your relationship with customers, in addition not to delivering real sustainable value for your customers.

Thus, SII tend to have 3 major disadvantages :

- High competition
- Lack of financial sustainability
- Loss of credibility

In other words, this type of opportunity lead your business to a red ocean (symbolic market where companies kill themselves because of cost driven products/services) Therefore, if your service segment is still small and lacking of competitors, you will achieve very interesting results by attending this sort of customer in a short term.

On the other hand, segments where the competition is high force you to innovate or quit. Both of the cases are likely to happen and it has already taken around 80% of companies out of the game during the first 2 years since their foundation.

Therefore, I will teach you how to dive deeper to reach the second type of innovative opportunity.

Figure 1

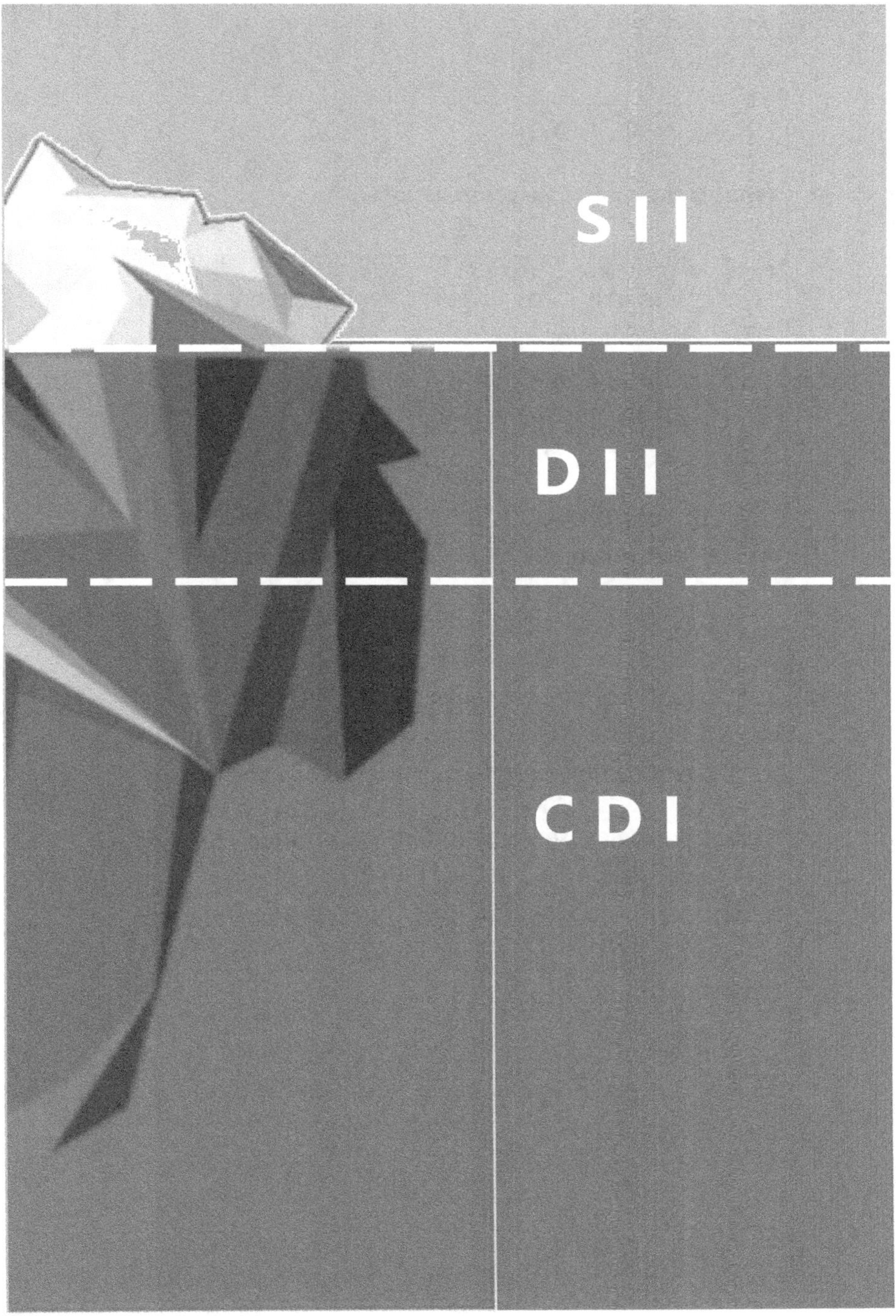

SII
DII
CDI

What is the main characteristic of DII?

- Requires short term empirical or practical research to create improvements and optimizations
- Bring highlight for your products
- Might imply on either patents or industrial design

This sort of innovation often consumes more time, money and resources to be developed. In addition, it also requires experts in the field to be rapidly implemented.

It is possible to see that for each significant SII, we can find 20 significant DII. And it makes the second piece of the iceberg 20 times bigger than the tip of iceberg.

Thus, the magical secret is to find the strategy that will reach innovation in this level. Obviously, the tools which are used for the first type are completely different from the tool which are used for the second type of customers.

Let's make an illustration, to find rocks on the tip of iceberg, no diving equipment is required. In this case, you do not even need to know how to swim.

Now on the second piece of iceberg, some techniques are required. You will have to know how to swim and sometimes use diving mask to reach submerse rocks.

Ok. What techniques I can use to deliver creative and innovative solutions to my customers? I will show you those tools later in this book. Moreover, I tell you in advance that this techniques are simple, but difficult.

How is that possible? You must have been asking yourself.

I will explain to you. Imagine that you want to train to run a marathon. That is very simple because there are tons of apps which can help to know what is needed. Nonetheless, it is not easy, isn't it? It is very hard because you will have to spend quite much energy, dedication and time on the training in order to be prepare to run the marathon.

Let take a look in the advantages of the DII:

- They are found in large scale and more significantly (often implying cn Patents and Industrial Design)
- There are less competitors fighting for them
- Therefore, the innovation price start not being the deal breaker and you can increase your profit margins in order to invest in your business (labor, equipments, technologies, et cetera)

On the other hand, what are the disadvantages of DII?

- You will need high profile technique and energy to identify , develop, materialize and deliver such innovation to the end chain

Alright, here you can see that there are disturbances and barriers that disturb you in the process. So, if you want to dive deeper and explore the larger part of this iceberg, thing will become even harder.

In the case you aim to reach an unbelievable larger group of opportunities, let's go deep and understand the third type of innovative opportunities.

2.3   Continuous Disruptive innovation (CDI)

What foments Continuous Disruptive innovation?

- CDI is fed by constant fuel
- CDI can rise from all the pores of organization, even from places that are not looking for it.
- CDI will create things that customers were not looking for, despite of their need

For example, there are people who need to take care of their health even though they do not know what is needed to do so. Likewise, there are organizations and people who need innovation, but they do not know what they need yet.

In this case, each opportunity from the tip of iceberg (the first part which every competitor kills to have) correspond to 50 CDI.

What are the benefits of CDI?

- They are found in even larger scale (50 -CDI per each SII)
- This segment has even less competitors, and sometimes monopoly because of patent
- Therefore, as your business will be driven by the innovation which the customer sees, you can increase you profit margins up to a fair cost

As the 1st and 2nd type of opportunities, CDI have their disadvantages too:

- You will need to apply even more energy, patience and high profile techniques in order to reach them

Well, talking by experience of who discover an strategy that actually works, I always aim at the DII and CDI. Apart from the moments that there are no competitors, I almost never dispute the SII because these moments are rare.

It is amazing to develop either DII or CDI because , it those zones, I barely have competitors . In addition, I can offer disruptive solutions, making the customers extremely happy, offering suitable techniques and obtaining huge profit margins.

Now that you know how to reach this two type of customers (DII and CDI),you will need to understand the 2 models of innovation generation.

3 The 2 models of Innovation generation

Every business, no matter what stage it is in (either the one who are taking baby steps or the giant of the market), wants and need to have more customers.

But, to achieve this, what is usually done? People invest in equipment, marketing, labor and infrastructure in order to deliver a differentiated service or product. In other words, it is common sense that it is necessary to differentiate services/products and improve productivity to bring more customers and create loyalty relationship. And, of course, you want that, don't you?

3.1   Branding innovation

When the matter is about innovation, the image which appears in our mind usually look like this:

A huge Innovation institute (like Nasa or Google), fulfill by labs, geeks and people wearing white coat all around. In the backside of this Innovation institute, a pair of robotic arms move object from a conveyor into an automatic chamber. In the frontside, people are having creativity sections in funny colorful room where people can sit in puffs and there is even a slide rising down from the top floor to the middle of room.

Did you see the image? Alright.

In this approach, the environment and resources are the predominant part and as a consequence, it works as innovation advertising besides the innovation generated. By chance, the customer will be happy by the final delivery it receives. This approach is called *Branding innovation.*

The main problem of this approach is that you have to invest quite much money in order to start having good results. And the worst part is that it is very hard to measure the gains and loss of this investment.

Why is this a problem?

Because your investment become an amortization amount into your fix costs whereas your customer does not expects to pay for this investment. In the customer's mind, your innovation is nothing but your obligation.

In contrast with giant companies, small and medium size businesses have not got millions dollars to invest in innovation institutes. They have tight budgets and each invested penny need to be paybacked in order not to jeopardize the business itself.

Of course, it is know that big companies such as Google, GE, Boeing and GM, invest millions of dollars in innovation labs and branding innovation. On the other hand, some companies count with geniuses in order to create innovation and branding innovation, such as Apple (Steve Jobs), Tesla (Elon Musk), Facebook (Mark Zuckerberg) and Amazon (Jeff Bezos).

And does this approach work?

Yes, it does. Otherwise, they would not have been doing it.

The most difficult part of it is the fact that these companies generally underuse their potential and do not know the actual gain obtained from their innovation branding.

You, as either a engineer, hobbyist, designer or the owner of a small/medium business, cannot afford to spend tons of money in such investment. Thus, you have to avoid the glamour of company like Google.

Ok. You have been imagining : I just want to make some research and get the millionaire idea. Some startups have already done that and it is different from innovation branding, isn't it?

Unfortunately, it is exactly the same. The focus in this case is the resources you need to implement that. And when you realize, it becomes a snowball that enticed you in a price that is so low you cannot pay your business fixed costs.

Therefore, you need to be more efficient from the point zero on. The **Customer Driven Creativity** is the clever answer for this dilemma .

Please, do not get me wrong. I am not saying that Branding innovation does not work. It works in two scenarios. 1) In the long term, after continuing spending quite much money without payback expectations. 2) In very short term without any competitors.

Nevertheless, none of those cases fits most of entrepreneur, small and medium business or even people. In my opinion, starting business requires that you work hard to ensure that each invested penny become a positive ROI in a sustainable way .

And how can you do so?

In order to better understand how you implement that, you will need to understand what is customer driven creativity.

"Quality is not what happens when what you do matches your intentions. It is what happens when what you do matches your customers' expectations. "

Guaspari

In this approach, the resources and technical elements are not as important as the impact that your idea/innovation cause on the customer expectations. Therefore, it is possible to say that the most important part of this approach is to put the customer in the stage, instead of equipments.

Thus, the metric into this approach is directly driven by the return of investments (ROI). In other words, the main idea in this concept is to identify how much the customer is willing to overpay because of the final result of your innovation. In this case, we will call it **perceived innovation.**

In the customer driven creativity , you can measure and directly correlate the **investment** and the **perceived value**.

I will exemplify this using a personal experience. In my first business, I have invested $100.00 up to $100,000.00 and achieved 20% ROI.

Do you want to know how I did that?

I created a virtuous investment cycle which works in this way:

Map things(features) that people like in commercial unique products, such as design, technology stuffs, surface finishing, material, et cetera.

At the first time, chose 2 or 3 very simple features to evaluate and implement. Note that the main goal of the first interactions is not to generate revenue, but understand how it works.

In order to identify these features, you can use friends, clients, and complete strangers. Note that you don't need a marketing research to identify these characteristics.

I started into an appliance store in a shopping mall. Imagine the situation, I pretend to look at some products while I was listening to other customers to talk about product. After that, I (fake) complained about the same features (talked before) and identify the reaction. The reaction people had was to defend their idea(product) and it often exposes the hidden perceived value of customer.

In my case, I began with 3 feature incremental features (Metallic cover, shot blasting finish and polish finish). For plenty of people this features are too basic, for other it is not. Anyway, I was comfortable to develop these features back in the days.

As this approach aim to measure profits, revenue and results. The definition of a budget make it realistic and tangible, instead of a non-refundable R&D program.

In my case, the first investment I made was $100 ($33 per feature). Certainly, it might be too much for someone, while it is not a big deal for others. It was an ok value for me at that moment. Moreover, the most important thing you have to think in this case is to define a budget to start the process.

Therefore, recommend you to define an small budget at the first rounds.

In this case, most of features can be implemented by either simple or advanced techniques, which consequently cost different amounts.

At the first interactions, use small budgets because the main goal is to identify perceived features (features that increase the value that the customer is willing to overpay).

Step 4

Measure the impact of features

In this step, you will realize that some features imply on better results than others. In other words, it means that each feature causes a different ROI.

Therefore, It indicates the first direction in the way of increase of perceived value.

Step 5

Redirect the investment/energy from the worst features to the best performed features

Using a metric (perceived value / budget) you can rank the features which performed the best. Thus, cut-off the last place and increase the investment of the first place.

In my case, I invested $100 and implemented in products that returned $300. So, I separate $200 of those and add in the my next budget. As a consequence, the next budget sum up $300 to develop and new value features.

Back in the days, I repeated all the steps using the new budget ($300) . And believe, it generated profit of $1000, at the moment.

Steps 6 and 7 might look obvious, but you would nearly fall off your chair if you realized how many people who do not follows these steps.

Just to illustrate it to you. One day I met one student of mine. He was part of a course I lecture which is called Make It Stunning. He told me that he had invested more than $200 in some strategies that returned $2000.

Terrific, isn't it? Of course!. So you imagine that he took advantage of this great development and increase his budget. Wrong! He used exactly the same $500 as the budget of the next development.

In my opinion, it was a classic strategic mistake. However, Master customer driven creativity is not enough to reach DII and CDI. For that, you will need to understand another strategy, **The quality driven creativity**.

In this approach, the customer continue playing a key role; nevertheless, the development of innovation imply on deeper and more effective ways.

Usually, the innovation generated by this approach results in Intellectual property, such as Industrial Design, engineering designs and Patents. Therefore, it is possible to see that this sort of innovation also brings the benefit of monopoly of a market/industry segment.

Although this approach is wonderful, there are very few companies or people which adopts this approach.

Why ? If this approach appears to be so good?

The main reason is because this approach is extremely hard to do without the right tools. In addition, this approach also requires quite persistence, consistence and insistence.

But don't worry. I will teach you all the tools that you need to implement such amazing creativity approach.

Therefore, remember that as I told you before:

This approach requires you to spend a lot of energy and practice in order to be effective. Otherwise, only the awareness of those tools will not help you to get results, but knowledge of this world.

"Quality is more important than quantity. One home run is much better than two doubles. "

Steve Jobs

4 Quality driven creativity

As you saw in the last chapter, Customer driven creativity was created to measure , improve results and boost impact of value feature on customers. It obviously help you to develop SII (Shallow Incremental Innovation), which goes right to the point.

These features might increase the perceived value in either a incremental or a sensible way. In other words, depending on the type of feature and strategy that you use, the results will be bigger.

In the group of the strategies which imply on sensible perceived value, a couple of step were included into the process in order to boost results. This strategy is called Quality driven creativity.

Let me explain it better to you.

In the classical approach, you produce increamental innovation and deliver to the customer in a direct way. So, the perceived value is included into service in only one step.

On the other hand, the quality driven creativity affects the 8 dimensions of **perceived quality** (elements in which customers see that worthwhile to spend their money) in **just 3 steps**.

1) Improve perceived features
2) Improve support and productivity
3) Give one step on the direction of breaking a paradigm

Ok. Now why is it a game changer ?

Because in the previous case (Branding Innovation), you blindly develop innovation features and then try to sell the whole idea to customers and investors:

-There it is amazing brand new technology that I have been developing for 2 years, but it is still in MVP (minimum valuable product) phase. It is a robotic system that place bricks on the wall inside construction site. Do you have interest in buy, use or invest?……..

-No, I do not.

-Ok. Bye.

Unfortunately, this approach did not bring a good ROI. Then, we had to invest the equipment, optimize machines, upgrade sensors, make the technology beautiful and invest in infrastructure. After working hard and present a new solution for the customer. What happened looks like this:

-There it is amazing brand new technology that I have been developing for 2 years, but it is still in small production phase. It is a robotic system that place bricks on the wall inside construction site. It is fully automatic, equipped with Artificial Intelligence and vision system and touch detection for safety. The operations speed can reach 1G and might increase production of walls in 50%. Do you have interest in buy, use or invest?........

-No, I do not.

-Ok. Bye.

This approach might work well for SII (Shallow Incremental Innovation), because who already knows about the technology will identify the value which your innovation brings. But on the other hand, they will force you to the edge, reducing costs and progressively raising their rule. This sort of customer are usually habituated with branding innovation and innovation institutes. In addition, their big companies usually have their own innovation laboratories.

Nevertheless, this approach does not work for DII (Deep Incremental Innovation) and CDI(Continuous Disruptive Innovation).

Applying quality driven creativity, you build a strong relationship with potential and current customers. In this case, you over deliver to your customer without charging a penny.

Another interesting point in all of this is the fact that Quality driven creativity increase perceived quality in only 3 steps, in addition to building another very important asset: direct and indirect partners.

Well, why does this sort of approach work so well?

For better understanding , let's remember the 3 types of innovative opportunities

- Shallow Incremental Innovation – SII
- Deep Incremental Innovation – DII
- Continuous Disruptive Innovation - CDI

Do you also remember that each SII correspond to 1/20 DII and 1/50 CDI?

Thus, Quality driven creativity targets exactly the portion of DII and CDI.

It happens because the customers that consume DII and CDI do not want to consume instantly. They want to you to help them to develop and launch their own IDEAS.

They do not want to spend money on work that you put on their ideas at the beginning. But, after you help them to maturate the idea ? or After you help them to create a stunning feature, such as a tactile texture, which will transform their idea in the product? Or even after they trust in your competence, productivity skills, organization and creativity?

Only after you build this relationship with the customer, you will understand their need and expectation. And when they decide to develop a new idea, product or service, they will not hire some no one who they don't know nor trust. They will develop the idea with the one who developed since the beginning.

On the other hand, creating this type of relationship help you to increase your development power, whereas the ideas which you develop with your customers works like a creativity section.

I will give you one example of that for you to understand better.

Imagine the picture:

A store owner hire a genius painter (a genius in the level of DaVinci or Raphael) to help him to paint his store.

Before starting, the man give the painter the blueprint marking exactly what is the color and paint which the painter should use.

The change of the man being satisfied is statistically minimal. Because he had hired a genius which delivered a work which he could do himself.

A better way to achieve success in a case like this would be:

The genius painter help the shop owner to understand architectural concepts.

 After identifying the expectations and needs of the man, the design is elaborated altogether. As consequence, the product plan is created and the benefits of the concept is significantly better than the first raw and abstract idea from the beginning.

Therefore, the store owner can hire the painter to make the design without hesitation. The painter produce a master piece which will make the owner happy.

Does it make sense for you?

If it makes sense, hold on, because now we will learn everything about the 3 pillars of Quality driven creativity:

1) Creativity tools

2) Perceived Quality Tools
3) Management and Productivity tools

"If you have always done it that way, it is probably wrong."

Charles Kettering

5 Creativity is not an state of mind, is it?

As you saw in the last chapter, Quality driven innovation is the step further in order to create impact and reach DII (Deep Incremental Innovation) and even CDI (Continuous Disruptive Innovation).

It is interesting to note that both customer driven creativity and quality driven creativity put the customer as an important piece of a complex beautiful machine.

Collecting data from customers are excellent tool to guide your next steps in the perceived quality and decide how to prioritize your investments.

Anyway, the process of collecting data and develop the relationship with your customer in order to create innovation and perceived quality is a hard work. The path and ability of developing ideas is called creativity.

As a consequence, the creativity can be indicated as a result of thinking mindset and mind cognition. because of some stimulus. In the case of innovation, the stimulus usually come from a problem or opportunity. That is the reason why the creativity is sometimes correlated to problem solving.

Therefore, this mindset and mind cognition separates geniuses from the rest of the human kind.

That is true, but it is not an absolute law.

Experts around the globe have been studying the behavior of creativity and problem solving processes for long time. As a consequence, a branch of the TRIZ disciplines which was created by Genrich Altshuller, identified 2 main types of creativity processes: Non Systematic Creativity and Systematic Creativity.

5.1   Non Systematic Creativity

The non-systematic creativity is a process in which there are no defined workflow to control the process of ideas generation.

Most of geniuses tend to follow this approach because their mind works a way that their cognition connects very distant points.

On the other hand, this approach is not exclusive of geniuses. Everyone has to work it own cognition in order to stimulate its creativity.

Although there are no workflow for non-systematic creativity, we can highlight 2 main approaches for the problem solving and creativity:

5.1.1　Think inside the box

This approach is also called vertical thinking or convergent method and indicates that the solution of some problem is obtained by the existent knowledge and converges to 1 solution.

In this case, the problem solving process is guided by personal experiences and knowledge in order to restrict options and identify one solution. This approach is also represented by a funnel of Ideas.

5.1.2　Think outside the box

On the other hand, thinking outside the box is an approach where a basis knowledge will multiply the options and solutions. In this case, the method diverges from the "obvious" solution in order to generate different results.

In this approach, the main focus is in the "movement value" of the statement idea. In other words, the most important thing in this approach is to move from one idea to other idea, instead of judging or criticize the current idea (critical thinking).

Some studies indicates a couple of tricks in order to stimulate the parallel thinking or divergent thinking

1) **Random entry ideas** – indicates that any random image, word, sound or smell will trigger cognition and unconscious correlations. For example, check the sequence of the first random word that you think after hearing another word:

   nose, toes, tooth, clean, white, medical coat, mask, surgery, blood, red, wine, glass, drink

   After some time writing or talking aloud random words, concepts start concatenating each other and ideas can be combined in order to create new ideas.
2) **Provocation ideas** – is used to move your mind to another direction in a well established wrong or impossible solution. The idea of provocation is to make your mind to exercise ideas to support exaggerations, idea reversal, escape, distortions and arising.
3) **Movement Techniques** – is focused in how to move to a different idea. In this case, it can be used the extraction of principle, focus on differences, highlighting positive aspects of problem of previous solutions.
4) **Challenge** – instigate new ideas through the simple question why? It is important to note that why? Need to be in a non-threatening

way, like a child, when trying to understand a new concept.

5) **Concept Formation** –intend to generate ideas by the comprehension of existent concepts. It can also be called benchmarking.

6) **Disproving** – Assumes that majority is always wrong (as suggested by Henrik Ibsen). Therefore, this approach establishes that if some idea is obvious, you should question it and take the opposite point of view in order to convincingly disprove it.

7) **Fractionation** – is a technique that consists in explaining the problem statement from different point of view. As consequence, each point of view might lead to different cognitions, correlations and different solutions.

New approaches also identify the combination of both methods in order to stimulate differentiated solutions in a existent knowledge. This approach is also called divergent-convergent thinking or double diamond.

Figure 2

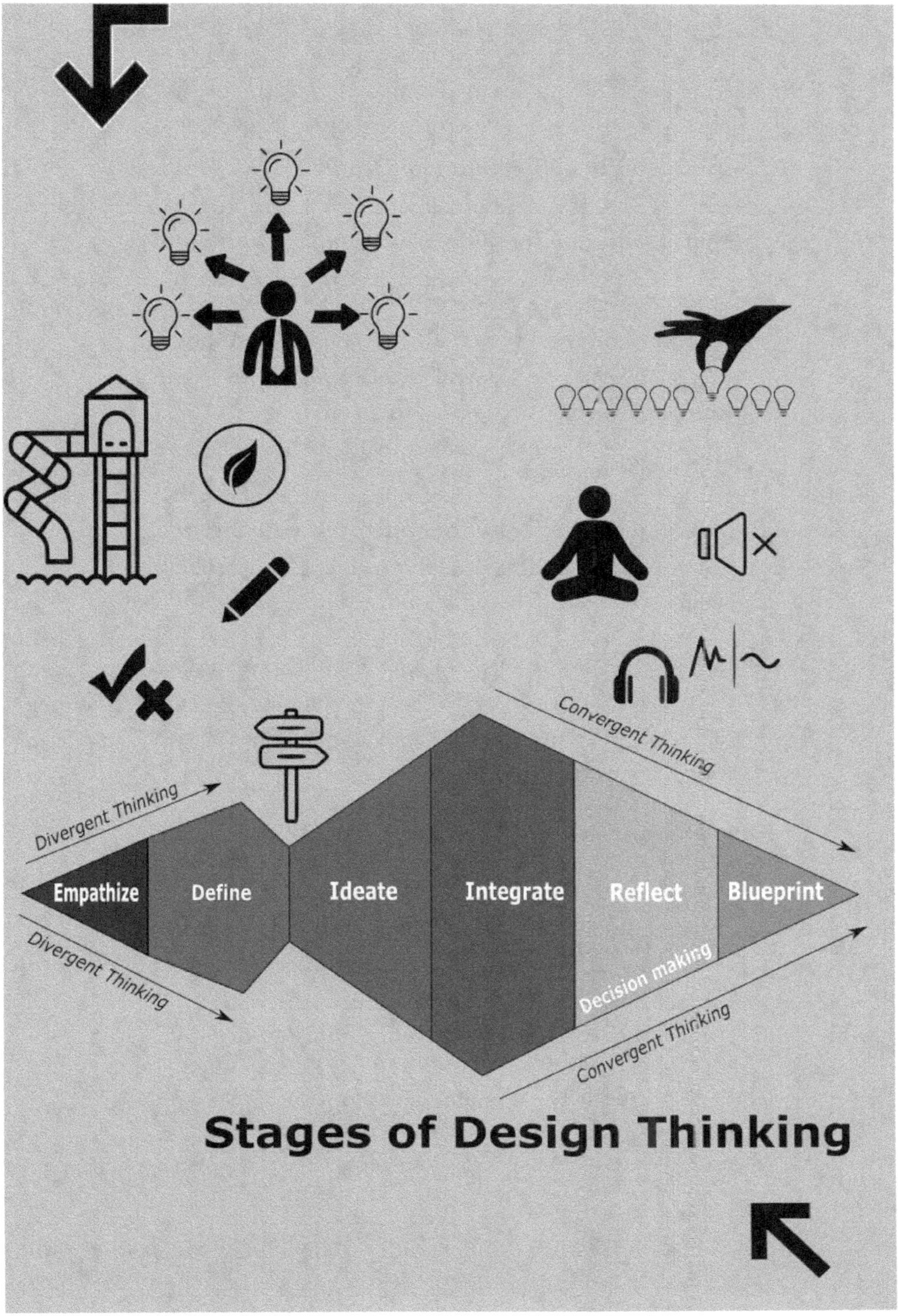

Stages of Design Thinking

Divergent Thinking

Divergent Thinking

Convergent Thinking

Decision making

Convergent Thinking

| Empathize | Define | Ideate | Integrate | Reflect | Blueprint |

Apart from the approach adopted for non-systematic creativity, several resources are used in order to amplify the results and stimulate the brain cognition.

Among the several resources that it is possible to incorporate in non-systematic creativity methods, I selected the ones that have indicated very good results in companies which are known to be creative.

5.1.3   Environment

The work environment is one of the key factors that helps to stimulate brain cognition, focus and problem solving.

In this way, it is possible to indicate plenty of startups which create environments where collaborator can relax, work in casual colorful funny place and even play during the working journey.

But why do they create such environment?

As commented before, parallel thinking can be stimulated by the principle of **Random Ideas**. Therefore the diversity of colors, shapes, images and even sounds introduce such principle in the environment.

Additionally, relaxed and funny environment triggers other 2 creativity stimulus: **Provocation ideas** and **Challenging**.

5.1.4 Noise versus focus

On the other hand, methods of productivity indicates that convergent creativity is amplified by focusing methods.

In this case, each individual have a different approach to increase productivity and focusing in any task. Therefore, there is a large discussion about the benefits of noise and silence for productivity and creativity.

For that reason, we will show you the most used life hacks that can help you to amplify convergent creativity, productivity and focus.

Create background noise

In this approach, background noise is used to make you lose focus in the external. The main goal of this approach is to make that the random sounds of the induced background noise merge with the external sounds.

As a consequence, any sound that comes from the external sources are ignored by your brain, allowing you to increase your concentration in the task you are doing.

Another different approach is listen to music and podcasts. Nevertheless, this approach is only proof to be useful for divergent thinking, jeopardizing parallel thinking. In spite of the benefits of music and podcasts, listen them during another task make you lose focus in both of tasks.

Another drawback is the fact that you progressively lose focus in daily basis.

Don't let me wrong, I love podcasts and music. However, after testing this theory in myself, I realized the it I true.

Total Silence – noise cancelling

In contrast, a different approach indicates that removing the external noise source will imply on total silence.

This approach is very common approach used by writers, artists, engineers and designers.

In addition, plenty of successful executive adopt **meditation and yoga sections** during short periods of time, at least.

The benefits of this method is reported to be extended along hours, making this an excellent tool to amplify your creativity.

Another technological approach can be adopted during the daily basis. Of course, remove all the background noise is impossible in a real life. Nevertheless, **noise**

cancelling headphones bring you very close of total silence.

Exercise – walk

When you imagine someone thinking, what picture pop up in your mind?

In my case, the first image is someone walking in circles.

This classic image is not wrong indeed. There are several studies that indicates that exercises and walking increase endorphins. In a Stanford study indicates that when people are walking they become 60% more creative than when they are sat.

As a result, **Walking meeting** become popular in startup companies and even among some remarkaɔle celebrities, such as Steve Jobs and Mark Zuckerberg.

5.1.5　Trial and Error

Another non systematic approach is the popular trial and error. This approach is guided by the fact that each error produces new ideas that lead novel ideas.

The drawback of this approach is the excessive spend of energy which also consumes motivation.

Nevertheless, several cases can be found in history, such as Thomas Edson, which used trial and error in order to generate innovative products.

On the other hand, several references indicates that trial and error is very useful for design thinking flow.

5.1.6   Time and priorities

In order to stimulate creativity, book a periodic time in the daily routine has already been proof to increase creativity levels. It is reinforced by the principle of repetition.

Although the non-systematic creativity is very useful for the generation of ideas, solutions and even innovations, the results of this approach usually reach SII (shallow Incremental Innovation) or DII (Deep Incremental Innovation) because of the instability of this approach.

That can be explained because this approach rely on people mood and creativity spirit, therefore external factors such as environment, political situation and sports result affects the final result of this approach.

For that reason, different approaches have been developed in order to maximize creativity in a systematic fashion way.

In contrast with non-systematic creativity methods, systematic creativity is highlighted by workflow and group of guidelines that lead you on the path of creativity and innovation.

In general lines, systematic problem solving and systematic creativity can be divided in 5 stages:

- Establishment
- Understanding
- Generation
- Evaluation
- Definition

Therefore, this approach considers that the whole problem can be segmented in small parts which are simpler to solve. After solving the small pieces of the big problem, it is possible to put all together and complete the problem solving process.

As a consequence, the knowledge about the design problem increase during the development process, while the design freedom decrease.

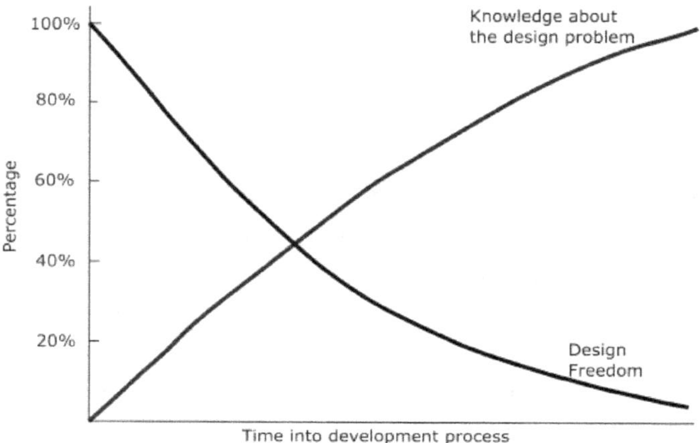

In order to follow this steps, it is often adopted creativity meeting where everyone who participates will be fully engaged in the problem solving process.

Another important point in this creativity meetings is the fact that the solution is a result of team work. In addition, everyone will have one responsibility in the meeting.

As a generic recommendation, several researchers define different title roles for team members in creativity meetings; Nonetheless, the most common roles are: Team Leader; Facilitator; Note-Taker; and Team Members.

In this approach, all the member need to be aligned, trained in the creativity tools and engaged in openly contribute for the problem solving.

Likewise, all the team members need to know that each team member is equal there are no experts nor "stupid" ideas during creativity meetings .

It is an important point because subject experts and analytical people are usually resistive and try to dominate the meeting.

For that reason, the team leader and the facilitator need to handle conflicts, criticizing, judgments and team members resistance. In addition, team leader and facilitator need to be stimulate and motivate the team members in order to achieve results, diversity and problem focus.

As a thumb rule, the stimulus are usually the same presented in section 5.1.

Table 1

Member	Responsibilities
Team Leader	-Organize the meeting
	-Define team members in order to provide different perspectives
	-Ensure that all team members are well trained in creativity tools
	-Ensure that all team members have suitable comprehension of problem
Facilitator	- Master creativity tools
	-Conflict management
	-Group dynamic management
	-Handle possible dominance of experts
	-Help progress of team when stuck
	-Establish schedule and timetable
	-Ensure followup of schedule and timetable
Note-taker	-Take not of all ideas in a literal way
	- Avoid paraphrasing or interpretations
	-Organize how team ideas will be collected: Flipchart, cards, boad, software, et cetera
Team members	- Agree in join the learning process
	-Agree in share experiences and point of view
	- Agree in be open to contribute with other members in sinergy
	-Commit not to criticize other ideas
	-Commit to avoid frustation because of process pace

It is important to note that this approach is highly associated to Divergent-Convergent Approaches, where the main goal of generation usually is to produce divergent Ideas, while Evaluation and definition tends to adopt convergent character.

Therefore, it is important that the team leader provides all the resources that are necessary in a creativity meeting. Depending on the stage of problem solving process and type of problem, different materials are necessary. Moreover, the most common **materials which are recommended in creativity meeting** are:

- Flipcharts
- Adhesive tape
- Markers
- Pens
- White boards
- Time for team members to be fully committed in the meeting, whereas the duration of creativity meeting might be long
- Desks and chairs for the team members
- Forms for the tools that require so
- Access to research, data, experts in accordance with the demand.

On the other hand, new approaches imply on new types of materials, and hackatlons, hackadays and hackanights are very good examples of new approaches of creativity meetings. Thus, materials for new approaches might additionally include:

- WIFI
- Access to Computer
- Specific Software licenses
- Event hashtag
- Training sessions
- Happy hours
- Access to workshop, techshop, makerlabs, Fablabs or equivalent simpler gear
    - E.g.: 3D printer FFF
    - laser cutter
    - 3D printer SLA /DLP
    - CNC router
    - Dremel
    - Drill
    - Hand Tools
- Basic mechanical prototyping materials
    - Sheets (Acrylic, plastic sheets Wood, ACM, Card boards, PS Foam)
    - Copper Teflon for PCB
    - Plastic Filament
    - UV Resin
    - Resin/Metallic Blocks
    - Glue / weld
    - Fasteners (screw, nuts, pins, bolts)
    - Sand paper
    - Aerosol Spray

- Basic electronic prototyping materials
  - Raspberries
  - Arduino
  - Basic electronics (Resistor, capacitor, inductor, Transistors, diodes, LEDS, mosfets, ETC)
  - Basic Sensors (Temperature, distance, light measurement, Hall effect , capacitor, potentiometers, tripod, force, etc)
  - Electronic Gears (Motors, servos, solenoids, compressors, Displays, etc)

Therefore, it is possible to see that these new approaches of creativity meeting are widely incorporated in several startup culture in order to accelerate the product development process.

As an example, the Dr. Alex Mehr, who is the CEO of the startup MentorBOX, implemented a very aggressive approach of product launching since 2007. In this approach, the main goal of an small group of developer is to launch 1 product per week. Effectively, Dr. Alex Mehr have more than 30 simultaneous working products generating revenue nowadays.

5.2.1 Establishing a problem or an opportunity ?

This stage consists in the identification of problems, complains, market gaps and opportunities.

It is important to note that you are not supposed to solve problems in this stage so that you will need to be strong at the first creativity sections that you will participate or organize.

In this stage, besides defining the obvious problem, it is important to explore the state of art in order to identify ALL the solutions addressed to the said problem.

Generally, the opportunities and problems rise as an answer to 4 basic questions:

- Are the current solutions satisfactorily working?
- Is the problem so critical that new and innovative solutions are required?
- Does the current solutions generate value for customer?
- Is the market so competitive that new products or new approaches are needed ?

Those questions tends to highlight gaps and market opportunities , whereas the obvious solution usually imply on high competiveness.

I will give you one example, Airbnb founders identified that the three most frequent concerns of travelers were:

- Prices
- Disconnection between City culture and hotel/hostel experiences.
- Difficulty of either booking or hosting

Because of these main travelers complains and answering the 4 basic questions, it was possible to identify that:

- The current solution was not satisfactorily working from the point of view of prices and customer experiences
- The current solution did not create value whereas it create difficulties for either guests and hosts
- The current market was so competitive that small businesses were swallowed by big hospitality organizations.

Note that in this stage, no solution has been identified yet and 3 problems / opportunities were identified.

Although there are not a straight line to identifying opportunities, several researchers indicates a group of creativity tools in order to stimulate and help to identify gaps and opportunities:

- Parametric analysis
- SWOT Analysis
- Systematic Patent searching
- Systematic bibliometric analysis
- Problem analysis
- Product-market matrix
- Portfolio matrix
- Blue ocean Value curve
- Ishikawa Diagrams (Root Cause Analysis)

You will learn how to use these creativity in the second part of this book, where is taught how to implement systematic creativity.

You should be asking now:

Ok, but after identifying the problem, what should I do?

Now is time to understand your problem or opportunity.

5.2.2 How to understand a problem or an opportunity ?

The second stage in the systematic problem solving approach, the main goal is to understand the requirement and uncovering existing solutions of similar problem. Additionally, the planning of how to solve the problem is also done in this stage.

In order to understand a problem, different methods can be applied in accordance with the type of problem to be solved. It is possible to use the same creativity tools which were used problem establishing phase.

- Parametric analysis
- SWOT Analysis
- Systematic Patent searching
- Systematic bibliometric analysis
- Problem analysis
- Product-market matrix
- Portfolio matrix
- Blue ocean Value curve
- Ishikawa Diagrams (Root Cause Analysis)

Nevertheless, this stage is most correlated with the **perceived quality**. Therefore, it is also indicated to use hybrid quality-creativity tools, such as:

- Quality Function Deployment (QFD)
- Analysis of 8 Dimensions of quality
- Blue ocean Value curve
- Perceived quality evaluation
- Six Sigma DMAIC
- The 8 Disciplines
- The 7 quality tools
- Function analysis

In addition, this stage also includes the planning of problem solving. Therefore, it is possible to use management tools to organize and identify process of problem solving (which can be considered a project).

Therefore, I will teach you in this book how to use the most effective and important tools that you can used to plan and organize either problem solving or innovation projects:

- Resources Assessing
- Scrum
- Sprint
- Gantt
- Project Tracing SpreadSheets

As understanding a problem will depend on type of problem that is expected to be solve, it is important to follow 3 steps:

- Collect Data
- Understanding Data
- Deploying Tasks

These three steps is almost obvious, isn't it? But you would probably fall of your chair if you have known how many people ignore these steps.

Imagine that the problem solving is an adrift car in the darkest night. This car has the lights off and you don't know where is the road and the night is so dark that you cannot see one inch ahead.

What is the first thing that you do?

Turn on the lights .

That is exactly what collecting data does in the problem solving process.

After being able to see the road, it is also important that you know how to drive, read map and read the signs in order to guide the car to the right direction.

In this example, reading the map and signs corresponds to understanding the collected data. In this case, it is important to identify where we are and where we would like to go.

The last step in this part of understanding the problem is to deploy tasks or planning problem solving tasks.

In our analogy, this last step correspond to analyze the map, sign and define what is the path to reach our destiny.

Note that in this stage, we did not tried to solve the problem because solving the problem w thout suitable comprehension of it is like driving an adrift car in the darkest night with lights turned off.

As this process sometimes is hard to be done at once. It is interesting to assess resources and competences which will be necessary to develop this opportunity (solve that problem). Likewise, it is also interesting to indicate what is the expected delivery obtained by this solve problem (opportunity).

Therefore, in order to plan the problem solving, it is always recommended to answer the 5W2H questions:

- **Why**?
    - Why is this problem need to be solved?
    - Why this opportunity is relevant?
- **What**?
    - What is the problem?
    - What is expected to be delivered?
- **Who**?
    - Who is going to do?
    - Who is going to collaborate?
        - Suggested heterogeneous group, different experiences and competences
        - Everyone need to be engaged and trained in creativity tools
        - No hierarchy difference. Otherwise, the highest level will dominate the creativity meetings
- **Where**?
    - Where is the project will be done ?

- **When**?
    - o   When the project will be done?
        - ▪   At a moment
        - ▪   Frequency
        - ▪   Period
- **How**?
    - o   How the project(problem solving) is going to be done?
        - ▪   Method
        - ▪   Tools
        - ▪   Tasks and Stages
- **How much**?
    - o   How much this project is going to take?
        - ▪   Resources
        - ▪   Investments
        - ▪   Human Resources
        - ▪   Dedicated time
    - o   How much is the return of investment?

After understanding the problem and planning how to solve the problem, the next step is to generate ideas.

5.2.3   How to generate Ideas ?

In this stage, the main goal is to create concepts, generate ideas and possible solutions for the defined problem.

In this approach, generating ideas tends to be similar to divergent creativity, where the general concept is to expand options and create new concepts.

It is important to highlight that you should not think about constraints in this stage because those constraints will be worked deeply in the next stage of problem solving.

It is also interesting to note the definition of problem can also be modified in order to stimulate new concepts and new solutions. Therefore, it is possible to use:

- Problem Reduction
- Problem Expansion
- Problem Digression

In order to create new ideas, concepts and new solutions for products or services, different creativity tools can be used in accordance with the Type and Relevance of problem in addition to the type of situation and resources available.

In this case, it is possible to separate the type of problems in 5 groups:

- Problems that require Analysis
    - E.g.: Requirements that a lamp must attend, such as bright level.

- Problems that require Solutions alternatives among a specific knowledge domain or Technology
    - E.g.: Type of energy source that generates light
- Problems that require new concepts or reconfiguration
    - E.g.: Mechanism that adjusts lamp bright level
- Problems that require selections among a list of known solutions
    - E.g.:The most cost-benefit material for lamp resistance
- Problems that requires evaluation of customer perception
    - E.g.: shape and aesthetic design of product
- Problems that require logic deduction
    - E.g.: Calculus of lamp efficiency (η)

On the other hand, choosing the suitable creativity tools depends on the type of situation and resources available. In this case, Table XX indicate suggestions of the most suitable creativity tools in accordance with the type of resource of situation available.

It is important to note that the recommendation of the creativity tools as a function of resources, situation and type of problem does not mean that other tools cannot be used. It just indicates the compilation of good results regarded during the years.

Another important point to be considered in the generation stage is the quality of desired solution. In this case, the creativity process must lead the team member to go beyond. Therefore, it is possible to identify the quality of ideas in accordance with the generalization level, which is also enhanced to the **abstraction level**.

Abstraction Level

The abstraction level is a metric that indicates how generic a problem, idea or concept might be described.

Let's take a Coffee Mug as example:

In the first abstraction level, it is possib e to see that the function of Coffee Mug is to hold coff≥e and keep it warm.

Alright!

Which other function this coffee mug might have in a second abstraction level? Does it only wo ks for coffee?

Thus, it is also possible to identify that the function of this coffee mug might be holding liquids and keeping it warm.

Going further. Does this coffee mug cnly works for hot/warm liquids ?

Alright! Therefore, we can identify in a third abstraction level that the main function of this coffee mug might be:

"Store matter in liquid and solid state in order to keep temperature".

As a consequence, higher levels of abstraction will lead to solution which are more different than the saddle obvious solutions.

Type of Situation		Creativity Tool	Problem that require analysis	Problems that require solutions alternative among a specific knowledge domain or technology	Problems that require new concepts or reconfiguration	Problems that require selection among a list of known solutions	Problems that require logic deduction
			Heuristic Redefinition Morphological matrix	Brainwriting 6-3-5 Classic Brainstorming Imaginary Brainstorming Analogies	Classic Brainstorming Imaginary Brainstorming Morphological matrix TILMAG Analogies	All creativity tools	None
Available time	Limited	Brainwriting 6-3-5 Classic Brainstorming		Brainwriting 6-3-5 Classic Brainstorming	Brainwriting 6-3-5 Classic Brainstorming	Brainwriting 6-3-5 Classic Brainstorming	None
	Wide	Morphological Matrix TILMAG ANALOGIES				Morphological Matrix TILMAG ANALOGIES	None
Team size	1 to 4	Heuristic Redefinition	Heuristic Redefinition			Heuristic Redefinition	None
	5 to 8	Classic Brainstorming Imaginary Brainstorming Morphological matrix TILMAG Analogies	Morphological matrix	Classic Brainstorming Imaginary Brainstorming Analogies	Classic Brainstorming Imaginary Brainstorming Morphological matrix TILMAG Analogies	Classic Brainstorming Imaginary Brainstorming Morphological matrix TILMAG Analogies	None
Team member relationship	experienced group	All creativity tools	Heuristic Redefinition Morphological matrix	Brainwriting 6-3-5 Classic Brainstorming Imaginary Brainstorming Analogies	Classic Brainstorming Imaginary Brainstorming Morphological matrix TILMAG Analogies	All creativity tools	None
	New group	Brainwriting 6-3-5		Brainwriting 6-3-5		Brainwriting 6-3-5	None
Conflict between team members	No	All creativity tools	Heuristic Redefinition Morphological matrix	Brainwriting 6-3-5 Classic Brainstorming Imaginary Brainstorming Analogies	Classic Brainstorming Imaginary Brainstorming Morphological matrix TILMAG Analogies	All creativity tools	None
	Yes	Brainwriting 6-3-5		Brainwriting 6-3-5		Brainwriting 6-3-5	None
Experience with creativity tools	Limited	Brainwriting 6-3-5 Classic Brainstorming ANALOGIES		Brainwriting 6-3-5 Classic Brainstorming ANALOGIES	Brainwriting 6-3-5 Classic Brainstorming ANALOGIES	Brainwriting 6-3-5 Classic Brainstorming ANALOGIES	None
	wide	Heuristic Redefinition Morphological matrix TILMAG	Heuristic Redefinition Morphological matrix		Morphological matrix TILMAG	Heuristic Redefinition Morphological matrix TILMAG	None
comprehension of problem	Limited	Brainwriting 6-3-5 Classic Brainstorming ANALOGIES		Brainwriting 6-3-5 Classic Brainstorming ANALOGIES	Brainwriting 6-3-5 Classic Brainstorming ANALOGIES	Brainwriting 6-3-5 Classic Brainstorming ANALOGIES	None
	significant comprehension	Heuristic Redefinition Morphological matrix TILMAG Analogies	Heuristic Redefinition Morphological matrix	Analogies	Morphological matrix TILMAG Analogies	Heuristic Redefinition Morphological matrix TILMAG Analogies	None
	Not	Brainwriting 6-3-5		Brainwriting 6-3-5		Brainwriting 6-3-5	None
Need to identify who generate the idea	Need to identify the author of idea	All creativity tools	Heuristic Redefinition Morphological matrix	Brainwriting 6-3-5 Classic Brainstorming Imaginary Brainstorming Analogies	Classic Brainstorming Imaginary Brainstorming Morphological matrix TILMAG Analogies	All creativity tools	None

5.2.4 How to select the right Idea?

In generation stage, no constraint were imposed and the main goal was to generate as many ideas as possible .

In general lines, a meeting of ideas generations tend to find up to 300 ideas. Nevertheless, not all the ideas is possible or worthy to be implemented.

For that reason the following stages of problem solving process is the Evaluation and Definition stages. In this stage, constraints start being imposed in order to create a funnel of ideas.

In this stage, it is important to follow a couple of steps in order to extract the maximum result from the presented tools of concept selection:

- Define problem constraints
    - Manufacturing
    - Costs
    - Implementation time
    - Implementation resources
    - Potential Return of Investment
    - Perceived Quality and Perceived Value of idea
    - 8 Dimensions of Quality

- Define weights and measurements
    - which constraint is more important to you

- o   Which constrain is available
- Classify Ideas/conception/solutions in groups
  - o   Similar ideas /concepts
  - o   Similar resources
- Select the suitable concept selection tool
- Apply concept selection tool
- Identity remove half of ideas
- Repeat process until you obtain 5 concepts

It is important to note that the tools I will present to you are extremely powerful. Nevertheless, the obtained results will depend on the quality of problem establishing and problem constraints.

Among the main group of concept selection and decision making tools, I will teach you how to use the 3 main types :

- Prioritizing Methods
- Valuation methods
- Experience driven methods

In the **prioritizing methods** the main goal is to correlate characteristics of concepts/solutions / ideas and problems constraints. Therefore, matrices, diagram and mind maps are used to evidence such correlation.

In the case of **Valuation methods**, the main goal is to measure the equity of operation, perceived value, and innovation valuation in order to select the concept which most generates value for the operation.

On the other hand, **Experience driven methods** are designed to identify and measure the effect of each concept on the customer experience. Therefore, this group of tools are usually enhanced to prototyping, mocking up, MFP (minimal functional products), MVP (minimal valuable products), MLP(minimal Lovable products) and User Experience (UX) techniques.

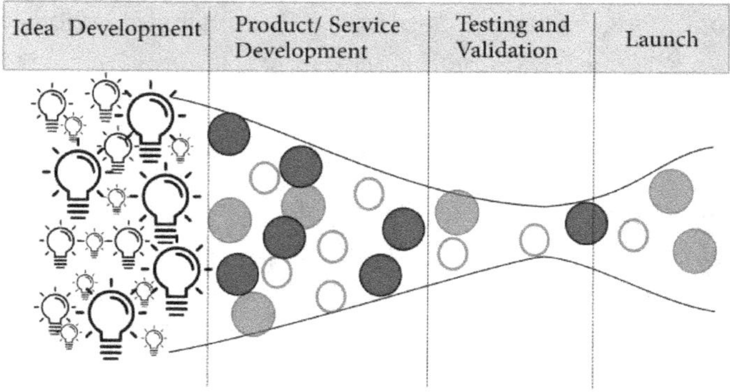

5.2.5   Why to use Development Approaches

In spite of the benefits of problem solving process, the path to innovation requires more steps to **transform the IDEAS in PRODUCTS or SERVICES** .

For example, imagine that you developed an amazing idea that could change the way of cultivating plants in urban spaces.

In this idea, you identified that urban spaces are small and people do not have time to spend in taking care of plants. However, you also identified that people in big cities value fresh pesticide free plants.

As a solution, you find that an automated urban farm which is controlled by robots would fit the problem constraints. People in small communities were identified to financially support the idea. In addition, it was regarded that this urban farms could be a next generation of lean distributed food cultivation, reducing logistics, producing according demand with high flexibility.

Ok. Amazing, isn't it?

Now, what are the next steps ?

Although great ideas are constantly generated around the globe, there still is a quite big stage between the idea and the product/service. Likewise, intellectual property and industrial design are also important factors to be considered in the development of new solutions. Otherwise, your new idea can be blocked by patents and penalized by royalties.

The next steps after the creativity process is the development process. In addition, this approach also is take in consideration because of the end of **product life cycle**.

Figure 3

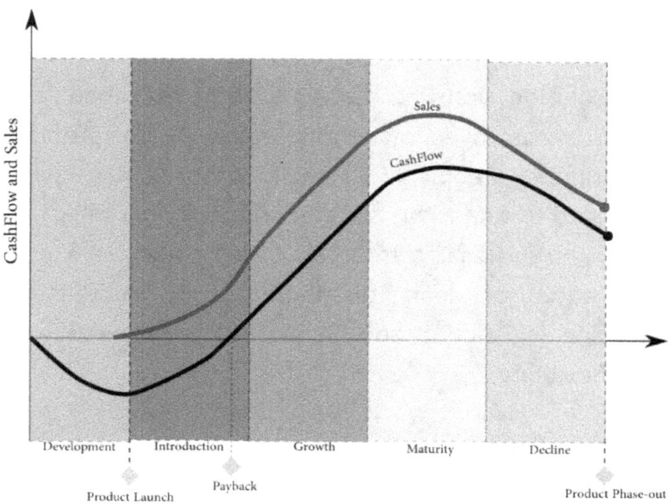

The Figure 3 presents the generic cash flow curve of a product during the life-cycle. In this figure, it is possible to see that the development only generates outcoming, while the revenue starts from the product/service launching.

After the sales growth and scaling phase there revenue stabilizes and it is possible to see and revenue plateau. The is the most important indicator in the product life-cycle, whereas the next stage is the product phase-out.

That is why several companies adopt product portfolio strategies where a new product is launched when an old product reaches the stagnation point.

Thousand of researchers have identified systematic approaches for product development, project management and services development. Those method depend on the type of product or service, having customized branches in accordance with the need of customers, team and company philosophy.

Moreover, I will show you the compilation of methods which express the most important development approaches in a simplified way.

I classified those method in 3 approaches:

- Product Development Processes
- Design Thinking
- Agile development

Among the product development processes, It will teach you about the general product development process in addition to the Development for Six sigma (DMAIDV).

As those methods are generalized, your implementation need you to adjust the process flow in accordance with your needs, your customers needs, your infrastructure and resources.

This type of development process is based on design and engineering of new products, even though this can easily be adjusted to development of new services.

Moreover, it is important to note that these methods enhance all the steps since the identification of opportunity until the product launching, e.g.: portfolio analysis, design and concept development, engineering development, manufacturing development, manuals and labeling, quality system and product launching.

On the other hand, different development approaches have been playing a new role in startups and corporate environment during the last years.

Design thinking and agile development are both methods that de-bureaucratize both product and service developments.

In both approaches, the development flow is highlighted by interactions and improvement in each interaction. In these cases, both open and close scope are adopted, even though open scope is the most usual.

It is also possible to highlight that agile development are very popular in software development where Scrum, Sprint and extreme programming tend to be the most used.

On the other hand, Lean startup and design thinking approaches are the most used in technology businesses where there are a mix of hardware, mechanics and software.

"A problem well stated is a problem half solved"

John Dewey

6 Innovation's Benefits

It is possible to indicate intuitively that innovation ideas lead to high competitiveness and improve market share.

However, I will show you that the innovation brings real benefits in addition to indirect advantages in companies, businesses and personal life.

In the book "Blue Ocean Strategy", Chan Kim and Renée Mauborgne describe several characteristics of companies that innovated and run away of red ocean (market that is driven by cost).

It is possible to identify that the blue ocean (market that is driven by innovation and gain of value) is more sustainable and gives companies a higher profit in addition to high customer satisfaction.

It is important to note that The blue ocean strategy does not indicates that the innovation or gain of value need to be disruptive. It need to be aligned with customer needs and customer expectations. Note that in several cases, the customers don't even know that they need or value something because they haven't actually known that thing before. Disruptive technologies are more likely to have this effect.

Likewise, disruptive innovation tends to walk altogether with intellectual property and Patents. It occurs because patents give the monopoly of the said invention (technology) to the inventor during 20 years.

Therefore, this is one of the best scenarios in businesses, having 100% of market share. And that is the strongest argument that supports intellectual property.

Of course, we can also indicate that intellectual property also protects your business to be copied, in addition to give you protection while you are still developing the idea and transforming it in a product or business.

In a small sphere, we can also indicates that an environment that stimulates innovation and creativity helps companies to overcome problems and crisis.

For example, McKiney and Company identified that among the companies listed in S&P 500 , the most **innovative companies performed 30% better** than the average performance of the S&P 500.

Additionally, it is also possible to indicate that companies that implements creativity environment and continuous improvement programs, such as Kaizen, have :

- Better productivity

- Safer Facility
- Higher quality
- Continuous cost reduction
- Continuous improvement of Communication
- Higher customer satisfaction
- Happier employees

Reducing the analysis to a personal sphere, it is also interesting to highlight that creative and innovative professionals perform better and achieve higher position then non innovative professionals.

Therefore, you have now plenty of reasons that justify you to move ahead and learn more about creativity, innovation, becoming an expert and generating value to your customers.

In the next chapter, you will learn about the most important tools that support systematic creativity and concept selection. In addition, this chapter will also indicates design and product development methods that will bring you to the cutting edge technique to generate continuous disruptive innovation (CDI).

2

Part 2 How to create and take advantage of a productive and creative environment

1 How to implement Systematic Creativity

Now you have learned that innovation and creativity are important components to any company, in addition to discovering that systematic approaches are more efficient and capable than non-systematic methods.

Therefore, I will show you how o implement systematic creativity methods into your daily basis besides your company.

The follow chapter will teach you the step-by-step of the most important creativity methods which are widely used from startups to giant corporations.

It is important to highlight that the following methods were divided in 2 groups:

- Creativity Tools
- Concept Selection and Decision tools

This division is based on the Convergent and Divergent Creativity and empower you to implement diamond and double diamond Creativity workflow.

As we are talking about systematic approaches, the following section will also introduce you to design methods and product development processes, such as:

- Design Thinking
- Scrum
- Design Sprint
- Product Development Process

Therefore, you will be able to implement such methods in a simple approach in addition to going deep in the state of art and specialize yourself in each method.

In parallel to creativity methods and design processes, there is always the quality development. Thus, I prepare a great compilation of quality tools which are extremely useful for you during development and creativity projects.

The last chapter of this book is focused in productivity and environment changes that will help you to modify your habits and become more productive and creative.

"Quality is more important than quantity. One home run is much better than two doubles. "

Steve Jobs

2 Creativity tools

Now that you learned about the importance of using systematic creativity methods, I will teach you either the most important or the most used creativity tools which remarkable companies successfully implemented.

I love hiking, and one important thing in this sort of entertainment is the quality or even existence of trails. Now imagine how it would be to hike a mountain without trails.

Hard, isn't it?

In this case, you would randomly walk around in any direction, if you have not had a good orientation.

Ok, but instead of walking around, consider that you study the best route through a map, mountain topography, environment on the surface and even a GPS.

It would be easier, wouldn't it?

Unbelievably, the obvious thing to do (define the problem before trying to solve) is always forgotten by the team members of creativity meetings.

Generally, people block their imagination and creativity simply because they have a fixed point of view of problem. As a consequence, they believe that there is only one approach to solve the problem.

This situation is usually called saddle spiral, where people got imprisoned in one or a group of ideas.

In the heuristic redefinition, the problem can be described by a system which can be compounded by subsystems or components.

Therefore, it is possible to understand the components as individual problems and afterwards put the solutions of each component altogether in order to solve the whole problem.

2.1.1   Definition

The Heuristic redefinition is a method that identify the problem as a system in addition to selecting the most suitable approach to create the effect on the system with the lowest effort. The approaches can be identified and ranked by implementation criteria and problem definition.

2.1.2   General overview

In order to understand all the point of view that a problem can be approached , it is necessary to identify all the possible problem definitions. As a consequence, the visualization of problem, their components and sub-components is usually more efficient when it is done by symbols, drawings, flowcharts or mindmaps.

Therefore, all team members can individually analyze the problem in order to answer what is needed to achieve the goal.

This **problem definition** is often in the form of a question:

"How we can ensure that ......?"

It is important to note that this method is usually indicated for problem definition, even though it can be used to generate solutions.

After **explode the problem in smaller problem definitions**, it is possible to evaluate the **implementation criteria**, such as **the level of difficulty** of each problem. In addition, the **time required to implement** each problem definition and **the impact of solving** them are also considered.

The correlation between the problem definitions and the score of Implementation criteria will help to identify which problem definition worthwhile to be solved.

2.1.3   Applying the method

This method is most indicated **for small experienced teams (1 to 4 members)** where the members have **wide experience in creativity tools**.

In this case, the **comprehension of the problem is wide**, even though new approaches are needed.

Likewise, this tool is more recommended for **Establishment and Understanding** stages of problem solving process.

Engineering and design problems are the most common application of this tools. Therefore, it is possible to explode the general problem (system) in small problems (components), in addition to address each component to a part of group to solve and develop.

However, this tools is widely used by individuals who aims to systematic analyze situations and innovative approaches to handle each case. For example, this tool is very interesting to self assessment and professional planning, whereas the problem definitions (Tasks, problems and opportunities) which will generate more impact on the career can be easily identified.

2.1.4   Step-By-Step

Step 1 – Establish the problem or opportunity in term of goals

Step 2 – Define the problem as a part of a system, including the main components

Step 3 – Identify each system component and its effect on the system

Step 4 – Establish the relationship between components and goals

Step 5 – Create a matrix which correlates problem definitions and established implementation criteria

Step 6 – Compare problem definitions and implementation criteria; ranking the total score

Step 7 – Discuss and select 2 problem definitions to be the most suitable problems to lead the team to a satisfactory solution

2.1.5   Examples

In order to exemplify the way that this tool works, we will use one practical example that we faced in our company 20 years ago. For the fabrication of plastic prototypes, it is very common to use silicone molds and liquid plastic resin.

One type of defect that might occurs in objects fabricated by this process is Bubbles or lack of infill.

Following the guide line of this creativity tool:

Step 1 – Establish the problem or opportunity in term of goals

It is possible to identify the absence of bubbles as an opportunity of goal to achieve.

Step 2 – Define the problem as a part of a system, including the main components

Therefore, defining the problem as a part of a system helps to identify the problems definitions in accordance with the 5W2H method:

- What happens?
- Where it happens?
- When it happens?
- Why it happens?
- How it happens ?
- Who causes the action? Who is affected by?

The elements related to the fabrication might be the main components that affects the problem.

In this case, it is possible to see that the main components that affects this process are:

- The mold Cavities
- Breath channels
- Air
- Liquid Resin
- Object Geometry
- Infill force (gravity)
- Bubbles
- Pouring process
- Temperature
- Humidity

In this example, answering the 5W2H, we can identify that:

- Bubble are made of air
- The bubbles occur during the pouring process
- Pouring process creates liquid turbulence that transport air inside the mold
- There is air inside the mold before pouring
- The air inside the mold is pushed of the mold by the resin through breathe channels and mold surface
- Air bubble often happen in flat horizontal surface imprisoning the air and generating bubbles

Step 3 – Identify each system component and its effect on the system

In order to identify the relationship between each key component, the team members individually find what is the importance of each component for the problem.

In this case, it is important to describe the relationship among key components. E.g.:

- Which components are have relationship?
- What affects the relationship between components ?

- Which laws or physical principles can be applied to describe the relationship between components?

Afterwards, the whole team discuss and answer **what each component does to affect the goal (positively or negatively).**

For example:

What the inside does in order to achieve the goal?

- The air is imprisoned in flat horizontal surfaces of mold (Negative)
- The air flows through breathe channel (positive
- The air is pushed off by the resin through the top surfaces of mold (air is always above the resin)

Step 4 – Establish the relationship between components and goals

Considering the understanding obtained by steps 2 and 3, now is the moment where we identify the problem definitions.

For that, we formulate the problem definition according to the follow form:

How can we ensure that ....?

Therefore, the team ask this question for all components in order to establish the list of problem definitions. In this example, the team identified problem definition for 10 components, Figure 4.

The first component, the question was related to cavity molds and it was also identified that the geometry of mold surface can imprison the air and generate bubbles. Formulating the problem definition

How can we ensured that **surface of mold cavities not to imprison air**?

Following the sequence of components, it is possible to identify the relationship between goals, key components and problem definition.

Figure 4

Component	Problem: How can we ensure that ....?
The mold Cavities	Mold cavities keep dimensions and integrity
Breath channels	lead air bubbles outside mold cavities
Air	flow out of mold
Liquid Resin	does not have bubbles
Object Geometry	does not trap air inside mold
Infill force (gravity)	push liquid resin inside small parts of mold cavity
Bubbles	explode duiring pouring process
Pouring process	does not generates bubbles
Temperature	is suitable during molding process
Humidity	is suitable during molding process

Step 5 – Create a matrix which correlates problem definitions and established implementation criteria

In this step, the team creates a matrix which correlates the problem definitions and establish implementation criteria, such as:

- The possibility of achieve the goal
- The difficulty of implementation
- Speed of implementation
- Expected impact of goal
- Total

The example of this matrix is presented in Figure 5

Step 6 – Compare problem definitions and implementation criteria; ranking the total score

After creating the matrix, it is time to score and ranking the components according an uneven scale.

In this case, it is interesting to use an simple scale with is up to 3 levels.

For example, the our team used 3 levels from 1 to 3, where:

- 3 points – Good/high
- 2 points – Medium
- 1 point – poor/low

It is not important to be sure about the score because this method helps you to point the direction of a solution.

Therefore, if you are in doubt whether the score is 2 or 3, try using all the doubtful scores up or all doubtful scores down .

Figure 5

Component	Problem: How can we ensure that ....?	The possibility of achieve the goal	How easy is to implement	How fast is to Implementation	Expected impact of goal	Total
The mold Cavities	Mold cavities keep dimensions and integrity	2	3	3	1	9
Breath channels	lead air bubbles outside mold cavities	2	2	2	3	9
Air	flow out of mold	2	2	2	3	9
Liquid Resin	does not have bubbles	2	1	1	2	6
Object Geometry	does not trap air inside mold	2	1	1	3	7
Infill force (gravity)	push liquid resin inside small parts of mold cavity	1	1	1	2	5
Bubbles	explode duiring pouring process	1	2	3	1	7
Pouring process	does not generates bubbles	2	1	1	2	6
Temperature	is suitable during molding process	3	2	1	1	7
Humidity	is suitable during molding process	3	2	1	1	7

3 points – Good/high
2 points – Medium
1 point – poor/low

Step 7 – Discuss and select 2 problem definitions to be the most suitable problems to lead the team to a satisfactory solution

The last part of this method is to select the 2 problem definitions which generates impact on the problem the most.

Based on these 2 problem definitions, the team discuss options and solutions to ensure that the components affects positively the goals.

From this phase on, it is very common that creativity meeting used different tools to generate ideas, such as Brainstorming or Brainwriting, among others.

In our example, the two most important problem definitions and components were found to be:

- Air –how to ensure that air find the way out the mold cavity
- Mold cavities – how to ensure that surface of molds cavities not to imprison air

Therefore, among the several solutions that the team identified to achieve both of problem definitions, it can highlight 3:

- Angle of object
- Position of pouring inlet
- Position of breathe channels

By the end, all those ideas were possible to be easily implemented and we solved our problem related to bubble traps in silicone molded parts.

2.1.6   Tricks and recommendations

Use a lot of perspectives to visualize the problem: One of the most common mistakes that people make is to see the problem from a single point of view.

The number of ideas and solutions depends on how much perspectives of a problem that you have.

Be patient, don't jump steps: Another common mistake in this systematic approaches is the impatience. As a consequence, people skip steps and try solving the problem without the suitable understand of problem.

If you define a problem wrongly, you will create solution for a wrong problem.

Think outside the box: A great recommendation for creativity meeting in the stage of understand, establish and generation is to think outside the box.

In this stage, it is not important to find or select the most suitable or cheap solution for a problem, but create alternative solutions for the problem.

A very good exercise to start thinking different is to get onboard dummy ideas, trying to justify them and creating new ideas that would help them to be possible.

"Others have seen what is and asked why. I have seen what could be and asked why not."

— Pablo Picasso, Pablo Picasso: Metamorphoses of the Human Form : Graphic Works, 1895-1972

One of the most famous creativity tool is the Brainstorming. Nevertheless, 87% of people which used brainstorming applied it wrongly. Alex Osborn analyzed causes of distraction and unsuccessful creativity meeting more than 60 years ago. As a conclusion, he created a guideline of behavior rules which was called Brainstorming.

The guideline was and is a success, nonetheless the results depends on:

- Use of collective knowledge to solve problems
- Remove of mind blockage
- Restraint of people critical sense
- Discipline to follow brainstorming rules and stages
- Participation of entire team members
- Avoidance of conflicts and unfocused arguing

2.2.1   Definition

The structured brainstorming is a creativity tool based on the generation of ideas in a non-judgmental open-minded space.

2.2.2   General overview

In general lines, the brainstorming is defined by 3 elements:

1) Create a team based on diversity and synergy .
2) Follow the rules and steps
3) Generate and Transcript ideas in a clear fashion way

It is important to note that each team member has a role. The basic roles are:

- Mediator
- Note Taker
- Team member

In this case, the mediator is the key gear of the machine, whereas each phase of idea generation need to be stimulated by. In addition, the mediator is the responsible for ensuring that the rules have been followed, such as conflicts and criticizing or judgmental comments.

The mediator is also responsible for the stimulation and motivation of team members, using intuitive and provocation techniques (see section 5.1 of Part 1)

2.2.3   Applying the method

This method is most indicated **for midsize experienced teams (5 to 8 members)** where the members have **wide experience in creativity tools**.

In this case, the **comprehension of the problem is limited**, even though new approaches are needed.

Likewise, this tool is more recommended for **Understanding and Generation** stages of problem solving process.

Problems which required new alternative, new concepts or new reconfiguration among specific domain or technology are the most common application of this tools. Therefore, it is possible to generate a large amount of ideas and concepts in a very small period of time.

2.2.4　Step-By-Step

Step 1 – Identify the suitable team members to perform the brainstorming session

Step 2 – Take all the members altogether in order to establish and make clear what are the basic brainstorming rules

Step 3 – Generate ideas

Step 4 – Clarify ideas and finish the brainstorming session

2.2.5   Examples

In order to exemplify how this method can be used. I will bring you a problem which was identified when I was manager in a company which has a big problem in the plastic manufacturing factory.

In this scenario, the problem was the fact that plastic parts got scratched before metallization (chromium-plating) process. Therefore, the scratch created uneven surface which jeopardized the product finishing. Therefore, the new product went scratched to the customer.

Figure 6

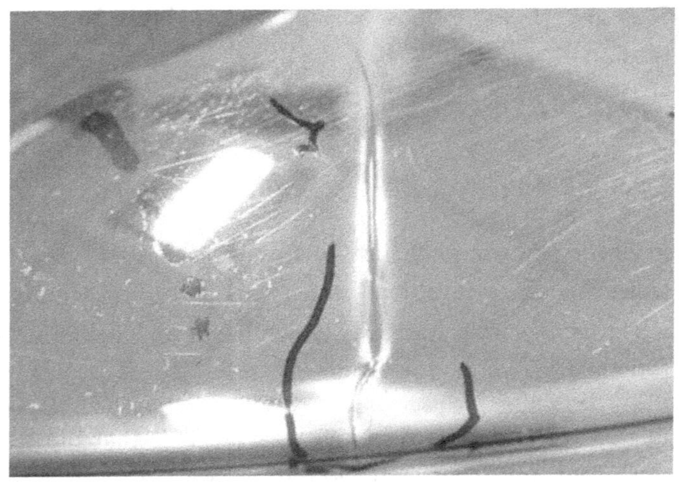

Imagine a similar situation, no one wants to buy a car which painting is scratched.

So, you can imagine the size of this problem in a factory, which was producing scratched products. It was waste of money and lack of respect to the customer.

Therefore, I decided to put an end on this problem.

Step 1 – Identify the suitable team members to perform the brainstorming session

I founded a creativity team which was called Quality war committee.

This group was removed from their daily duties and was composed by at least one representing member of each factory department. By the end, the number of members totalized 10.

In this case, the departments which were represented were:

- Supply chain
- Plastic manufacturing
- Product Engineering
- Quality control
- Painting and Metallization

Therefore, this multidisciplinary team was created with the main goal of solving factory problems and generate value.

Step 2 – Take all the members altogether in order to establish and make clear what are the basic brainstorming rules

There are 7 main basic rules in a structured brainstorming session:

Basic Rule 1 – You shall not criticize nor judge nor analyze whether a idea is good or bad, feasible or unfeasible during a brainstorming session.

The main goal is to generate ideas, instead of evaluate them. Therefore, this rule will ensure that:

The Ideas flow and association chain don't be interrupted

Discussions about pros and cons will be done in next sessions

This keeps participants motivated and protected from blocking triggers, such as sentences and body language. For example, follow a list of blocking triggers sentences:

- In theory this work but…….
- You will be responsible for that?
- We have that already!
- It does not work!
- It is too expensive

It is very important to note that body language and face expressions creates the same negative effect on the session.

Basic Rule 2 – You shall use your friends ideas to generate other ideas. It is important to note that a brainstorming session is an group effort and team member are not supposed to urge copyrights for their own contribution. It is important to note that **brainstorming session generate a collaborative creativity**. Therefore, if there is any award or compensation for the idea owner, all the team members should receive the same share of the award.

Otherwise, branches of an idea will create conflict among team members.

Basic Rule 3 – You shall release your imagination. It is very important to motivate and stimulate team members to let their mind flow freely.

All the team members need to be aligned with the idea and encourage their pears to go forward. Minor deviations might result in amazing results.

Of course that this freedom might diverge from the problem. Nevertheless, the facilitator need to handle the situation, incrementing ideas to the desired direction.

Basic Rule 4 –More is better !. It is important to note that this method goal is to generate as much ideas as possible. Therefore, it is important all team members to be in the same page. The goal is the quantity, not the quality of ideas.

The quantity of ideas ensure the cognition flow and idea generation process. Therefore, the thinking process become more spontaneous and unusual ideas are stimulated to rise.

Basic Rule 4 –You shall draw whether it is necessary. If one idea is popping up your mind, and you cannot describe it with words, draw.

The important thing in this case is to generate ideas.

Basic Rule 5 –You shall produce a safe space! In brainstorming sessions, it is important none to be introduced as expert or boss.

People become shy and embarrassed to share "dummy" ideas in front of experts or bosses.

Nonetheless, dummy ideas are exactly what brainstorming stimulate to transform in unusual approaches .

Basic Rule 6 –You shall keep sense of humor. Creativity sessions are supposed to be a joyful moment. And people in a good mood generates more ideas.

Basic Rule 7 –You shall not be in a rush. One of the most common mistakes that people make in brainstorming sessions is to underestimate the time that is needed for the brainstorming session.

As a consequence, team members become anxious because they have other daily tasks to do.

Therefore, suitable time need to be granted to all team members in order to dedicate to the problem solving and creativity session.

In our example, all team members were removed from their routine and environment in order to fully dedicate to the task force.

Of course, most of times full dedication is not possible. Nevertheless, separate a full day or a half day for each creativity meeting in advance so that team members can organize their schedule.

Step 3 – Generate ideas

In general, a typical brainstorming session begins with few ideas. After some time the number of generated ideas reaches the peak. Right next this moment, it usually occurs the first silent moment which is called **the first dead spot**. This marks the end of the first wave of ideas generation.

This often happens because the team members are thinking and it is normal that people take some time to think.

Whether the group does not restart by itself, the facilitator need to use different techniques to light the sparkle of idea generation again.

As presented in the first part of book in section 5.1, different provocations can be used to stimulate the brain to generate ideas.

For example, it is common that the facilitator ask the team members to play with some previous ideas in order to improve them and force less-active members to participate.

The second wave of ideas generations will probably generates less ideas than the first wave. However, those ideas are new and more creative than the ideas from the first wave.

As well as the first wave, each wave ends with a dead spot, and when the higher is the number of wave, deeper and more critical the idea will be.

So, when we should stop the session?

It is common that brainstorming sessions have up to 4 ideas generation waves, even though that is no rule indicating the minimal or maximal.

The important thing in this case is that the process need to finish before team members become either tired or irritated.

Figure 7

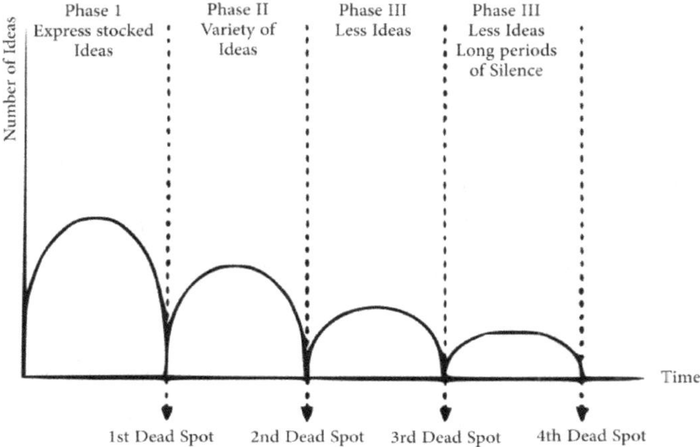

In our example, we can identify 50 ideas in the first wave, where the dead spot occurs in 10 minutes. The duration of second wave was 12 minutes and generated 23 ideas, while the third wave had duration of 5 min and 5 ideas.

Step 4 – Clarify ideas and finish the brainstorming session

In the final part of session or in other session it is important that team members to review the generated ideas in order to ensure that everyone understood correctly what the idea had meant.

This moment is not a analytic moment nor a moment to evaluate idea quality. It is just a moment where people clarify ideas to transcript.

By the end, it is also essential to expose to the team who and how their ideas will be evaluated by, in addition to expose the next steps and how the team members will be informed.

In our example, the solution we implemented was individual package during production in addition to handles parts using gloves and 100% inspection.

2.2.6   Tricks and recommendations

Choose a facilitator which is expert in creativity tools

Sometimes, team members struggle to have new problems insights. Either habitual paths or old solutions stick in the members mind and hold back the imagination and de generation of new concepts.

For that reason, a experienced facilitator plays an important role in the creativity meeting, whereas different techniques of creativity, provocations and imagination stimulations can be used to break down paradigm walls which team members might face during the brainstorming session.

Limit of team members must not exceed six

In brainstorming sessions, it is important to extract the maximum of ideas and experiences of all team members. For that reason, team members skills must be complementary each other.

In addition, groups which are larger than 6 tends to mute and inhibit less active members. As a consequence, these collaborators are underused and the main idea of brainstorming get lost.

If you have a large task force and want to generate ideas, divide the big group in small brainstorming sessions and you will obtain the double (n times) of the results.

Question Focus

It is very common that team members have different point of view about free imagination during brainstorming sessions. For that reason, there is a tendency of defocusing in these sessions. For that reason, the facilitator must help the team members to keep focus in the problem and goal.

It is important not to criticize but redirect attention to the problem in matter. For example, it is possible to use redirect questions such as: How this/that idea can directly help the problem ?

Don't let experts to lead

Another important point in brainstorming sessions comfort of all team members in respect to free their imagination.

In this point, all team members must ensure that any idea from anyone in the session is valid. No idea must be ignore. Nevertheless, it is sometimes difficult for the "experts in the field".

The experts in the field tend to be the know-it-all about the subject and several times tend to dominate the session, criticizing and analyzing with either words or body language.

On the other hand, the non experts become either dependent of experts or inhibited by the experts. In this case, the team members feel intimidated and embarrassed to give some dummy idea in front of experts.

Both of cases are extremely unproductive and the facilitator must sense this type of behavior very fast in order to avoid ideas blockage.

When an expert intend to dominate the session, analyze or criticize any idea (breaking the brainstorming rule), the facilitator need to moderate and redirect the focus to other direction.

It is important to encourage experts to generate ideas that make "dummy" feasible.

Don't go to deep

In spite of the common sense of brainstorming sessions, people forget to generate more ideas and start analyzing them.

That is a classic mistake that inexperienced teams make. The Facilitator need to constantly remember the team not to analyze because the analysis will happen in a further stage.

Clarify, don't criticize

If anyone don't understand an idea, it is very important not to analyze or criticize. It is important to clarify the idea adopting a group of pre-established questions or clarification action.

For example, it is possible to establish:

"Can you explain more in detail? "

"How this will solve the problem?"

"Learn the rules like a pro, so you can break them like an artist."

Pablo Picasso

Another alternative technique that obtain good results is brainwriting In contrast with the brainstorming, which is majorly performed verbally, this method is performed is performed in silence. In this case, all team members write their ideas on paper.

The most popular version of brainwriting is called Brainwriting 6-3-5 because it consists in 3 parameter: **6** group **members – 3 ideas** per round – **5 minutes** per idea generation round.

It is interesting that this method tend to generate a controlled amount of ideas in addition to allow team members to think through their peers ideas.

Advantages

1) In this method the participation is unlimited because of the numbers of member in each group.

 For example, imagine that you have a team with 12 members. In brainstorming, several members will be inhibited.
In the Brainwriting 6-3-5, it is possible to create 2 groups of 6 or 3 groups of 4 in order to perform the method. Everyone will participate and contribute their ideas.

2) the team members can formulate their ideas better, with no distractions nor discussions

3) The brainwriting generate absence of criticism because there is no discussion

4) Team members who are either non experts in the field or have low hierarchy position become more comfortable to contribute.

5) In contrast with brainstorming, brainwriting does not require an experienced facilitator because the session is self manageable.

Disadvantages

1) In the brainwriting, sharing ideas process is less spontaneous than in brainstorming.

2) In the brainwriting, the facilitator do not have chance to lead the discussion

3) In the brainwriting, some misunderstanding is hardly clarified

2.3.1   Definition

The Brainwriting 6-3-5 is a creativity method based on writing and silence to increase focus and creativity. In this method, the participants have defined time to generate theirs ideas in a controlled fashion way in addition to stimulate participants to understand peer ideas and produce synergetic ideas.

2.3.2 General overview

In this method, the general structure is based on writing. Therefore, each team member receive a ideation card (Figure 8) where they have to write down 3 ideas in a period of time of 5 minutes.

Figure 8

Problem:			Sheet: 1 date:
Round	Idea 1	Idea 2	Idea 3
1			
2			
3			
4			
5			
6			

After finishing the this period of time (round), the participants deliver the card to the next member counter clock wise or clock wise (need to be the same during the whole session).

Then, the next round starts and the participants have 5 minutes to read the peer ideas and write down their own ideas.

The process repeat until the goal amount of ideas is generated or until there is a round where no idea is generated.

It is possible to see the generation of ideas follows a gradual curve as a function of time, where 72 ideas are generated in only 20 minutes (4 rounds) in a group of 6 members.

Figure 9

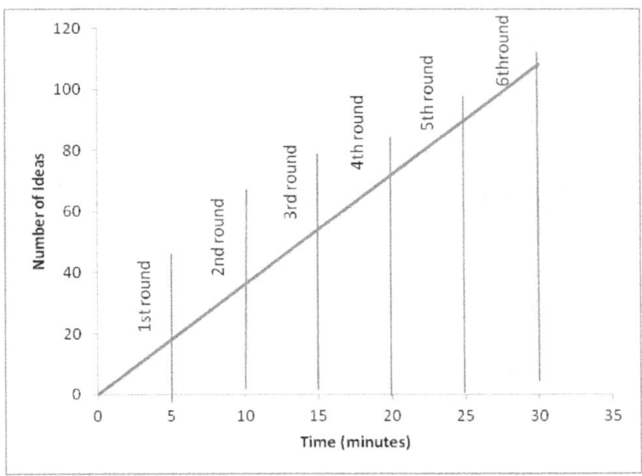

2.3.3   Applying the method

This method is most indicated **for midsize experienced teams (5 to 8 members)** where the members might have either **limited experience in creativity tools been**.

In this case, the **comprehension of the problem is limited**, even though new approaches are needed.

Likewise, this tool is more recommended for **Understanding and Generation** stages of problem solving process.

Problems which required new alternative or new concepts among specific domain or technology are the most common application of this tools. Therefore, it is possible to generate a controlled amount of ideas and concepts in a **very small period of time**.

This method is **extremely important** for teams where there are either **members with strong opposed ideas** or who are **experts** in some field and try to **dominate** creativity session.

2.3.4 Step-By-Step

Step 1 – Identify the suitable team members to perform the brainstorming session

Step 2 – Distribute ideation cards

Step 3 – Give instructions

Step 4 – Team members fulfill cards

Step 5 – Analyze ideas and select the most suitable

2.3.5   Examples

The example of Brainwriting 6-3-5 application we will present to you is related to the name of a course which we created several years ago.

The main goal of this course was to teach how to create new businesses based on 3D printing technologies. In addition, the type of customers which we intend to reach was customers non experienced in 3D printing.

Why this type of customers ? Because there are no competition about this type of customers and they are looking to engage in this type of business.

You can learn more about this in the book: "**How to use Advanced finishing technologies to increase your value and multiply your profit by 20**".

In this case, the problem was how to take attention of people that group of customers and still inform about the course content.

Then our team decided to use Brainwriting 6-3-5 to generate ideas for the course name.

In summary, the team was composed by 3 members and we spend 3 rounds of 3 minutes to generate ideas. As a consequence, we generated 27 great ideas in **less than 10 minutes**.

Obviously, larger groups in addition to further rounds will generate more ideas. And that is exactly the point.

Figure 10

Problem: Define name for course which attract customer who are not 3D printing experts and explain content of course (create business with 3D printing technologies		Sheet: 1 date:	
Round	Idea 1	Idea 2	Idea 3
1	How to create 3D printing Businesses	Take Advantage of 3D printing technologies	A to Z of 3D printing Startups
2	3D printing from zero to 1 million	From zero to 3D printing	Mastering 3D printing services
3	How a 3D printing bureau works	The ultimate guide for 3D printing businesses	Make money with 3D printing

Problem: Define name for course which attract customer who are not 3D printing experts and explain content of course (create business with 3D		Sheet: 2 date:	
Round	Idea 1	Idea 2	Idea 3
1	3D printing por enterpreneur	Incorporating 3D printing in your business	Take advantage of 3D prining
2	How 3D printing changed my business	3D printing for beginners	3D printing Money
3	3D printing 101	Innovate your business with 3D printing	how to design products with 3D printing

Problem: Define name for course which attract customer who are not 3D printing experts and explain content of course (create business with 3D		Sheet: 3 date:	
Round	Idea 1	Idea 2	Idea 3
1	Lauching products with 3D printing	Unveiling the secrets of 3D printing businesses	3D printing businesses naked
2	Selling 3D printing products	3D printing for startups	Start making money with 3D printing
3	How to innovate with 3D printing	Change your life with help of 3D printing	3D printing - Mastering the future profession

2.3.6   Tricks and recommendations

Establish limited generous time

In theory, 30 to 45 minutes of brainwriting 6-3-5 session generates 108 idea. Nevertheless, this number might be smaller because some members might write only 1 or 2 ideas per round. In addition, the first rounds might generate several similar ideas. Therefore, the total amount of ideas is reduced.

In order to avoid that, increase the standard round time from 5 to 7 minutes, for example.

Another strategy is to define progressive increase of time where the first round has duration of 3 minutes and the sixth round does 7 minutes. It makes sense because the team members need more time to read the previous ideas of card before write their own ideas.

Write ideas clearly

It is important to highlight that the ideas must be written in a clear fashion way so that the other team members can read and comprehend the idea.

Use digital resources and mobile devices

As we are in a digital era, it was impossible to let this feature apart.

One of the best advantages of brainwriting is the fact that this method is totally aligned with remote and virtual environments.

In this case, it is possible to use collaborative tools in order to perform a digital brainwriting 6-3-5.

I will recommend you a couple of the tools which I have already used.

- **Trello** is an amazing tool for agile planning, scrum and kambam. For that reason, it is possible to use virtual cards which move into the board in order to generate ideas in accordance with brainwriting rules.
- **Online brainwriting tools** are also very interesting and it helps to coordinate the creativity session, such as:
  - LucidChart

https://www.lucidchart.com/blog/how-to-use-brainwriting-for-idea-generation

  - Visual Paradigm

https://online.visual-paradigm.com/pt/diagrams/features/brainwriting-tool/

  - StormBoard
    https://stormboard.com/
  - StormZ

https://stormz.me/

  - IDEA Brainwriting

https://play.google.com/store/apps/details?id=com.ch maurer.idea

If an idea is hard to understand, draw

It is important to highlight that write an idea do not necessary need to be in words. It s possible to use drawing and flow charts in order to clarify the idea.

"Around here, however, we don't look backwards for very long. We keep moving forward, opening up new doors and doing new things, because we're curious...and curiosity keeps leading us down new paths."

Walt Disney Company

For me, the first time that I applied the imaginary brainstorming, I was really intrigued. As the name suggest, the imaginary brainstorming is a branch of structured brainstorming. Nevertheless, this method is marked by the **disproval principle.**

Using this principle, the problem becomes really weird and looks like different from the real problem. But surprisingly, the imaginary problem is strongly linked to the real problem.

For example, instead of engaging workers to clean their own workstation, it is possible to establish an imaginary problem: how to convince workers to wear costumes during the daily basis.

2.4.1   Definition

Imaginary Brainstorming is a creativity tool which help the team members to think outside the box in order to solve an imaginary problem which is radically different from the real but strongly correlated to the real.

2.4.2   General overview

In general lines, the imaginary brainstorming begins with the structured brainstorming. After generating ideas, essential problem elements are defined in order to define the problem.

Therefore, we replace these essential problem elements for imaginary problem elements. For example, the real problem was identified by the team as: "Ways to improve communication among departments". The essential problem elements were defined as "improve", "communication" and "Departments".

Applying the imaginary shift on departments, it is possible to establish the problem as: "Ways to improve communication with Martians ".

Therefore, the mind of team members shift and open to new perspectives, which can be applied to the real problem.

Afterward, a new brainstorming session is performed in order to solve the imaginary problem. Thus, the generated ideas for the imaginary problem are transformed to suitable ideas for the real problem.

2.4.3   Applying the method

This method is most indicated **for midsize experienced teams (5 to 8 members)** where the members might have either **limited experience in creativity tools been**.

In this case, the **comprehension of the problem is limited**, even though new approaches are needed.

Likewise, this tool is more recommended for **Understanding and Generation** stages of problem solving process.

Problems which required new alternative or new concepts or reconfiguration among specific domain or technology are the most common application of this tools. Therefore, it is possible to generate a controlled amount of ideas and concepts in a **very small period of time**.

2.4.4 Step-By-Step

Step 1 – Define the goal or problem

Step 2 – Generate ideas by structured brainstorming

Step 3 – Define essential elements for problem definition

Step 4 – Propose replacement of each essential element by imaginary surrogates

Step 5 – Radically replace one of essential elements in order to create the imaginary problem

Step 6 – Generate ideas for the imaginary problem by structured brainstorming

Step 7 – Transform ideas of imaginary problem in suitable ideas for the real problem

2.4.5   Examples

How to create project management tools with no resources ?

One example that my team and I applied Imaginary Brainstorming occurred when we have been looking for self management alternatives for an overloaded department.

This department was responsible for receiving, inspecting and approve all the components and materials that entered into the factory.

The problem was difficult to solve because there were more components to inspect that people to inspect.

Therefore, we decided to apply the imaginary Brainstorming.

At the **first step**, the team defined the real problem as:

"Alternative ways to receive and inspect more components per day"

The **second step** was to generate ideas using structured brainstorming. For example, we registered :

- Increase collaborators
- Reduce components
- Not to inspect
- Increase working journey
- Reduce quantity of inspection samples
- Borrow collaborator from other departments

Therefore, we defined the **essential problem elements** the **third step** in accordance with 5W2H (section 5.2.2). In this case, it was possible to identify that:

- The overload occurred seasonally
- There were components that were more urgent than others
- Each component requires a different among of time to inspect
- Each inspector can handle an amount of time per day

As you can see, there was not so bright insights from this brainstorming, mostly because the team was too involved by the problem routine.

As a consequence, our team simplified the essential problem elements as:

- Inspect time
- Components per day
- Priority components

In this approach, the problem become:

"How to maximize inspect time in order to deliver more priority components per day"

The **fourth step** was a tricky step because everyone is so involved in the role they are playing that it is difficult to think outside the box.

In this step, take a suitable time to create the imaginary problem.

In our example, we replace the context to a coffee house:

- Inspect time -> Food and drinks preparation
- Components per day -> number of tables
- Priority components -> First orders

Therefore, the problem become:

"How to make food and drinks faster in order to serve the first order in a full house "

Based on this statement, the **sixth stage** consisted in generate ideas to solve the imaginary problem, in the coffee house context.

In our example, different approaches were possible to be identified, such as:

- Use order queue
- Use a board with order sticks notes
- Start preparing the food/drinks that takes longer time to be prepared
- Prepare in advance part of dishes that are the most ordered
- Prepare the faster dishes first
- Deliver dishes partially, for example (if someone order start, main dish and dessert, the kitchen start preparing the starts)

It is possible to see that the ideas took a different approach and were very different from the ideas generated by the real problem brainstorming.

The last stage (**seventh Step**) consists in transform the imaginary problem ideas to real problem ideas.

We can use 3 basic approaches in this step:

- Use exactly the same idea
- Modify and transform idea
- Use the imaginary idea in order to obtain new real problem ideas.

As a result of the my team work in this example, we obtained:

- Use order queue was **transformed** in priority ranking (by severity)
- Use a board with order sticks notes was **transformed** in a Kanban Board
- Three ideas were transformed in heuristic queue rules:
    - Prepare the faster dishes first become – **Becomes** Shortest Job First (SJF)
    - Start preparing the food/drinks that takes longer time to be prepared – **becomes** Longest Job First (LJF)
    - Use order queue – **becomes** FCFS (First Come First Served)
    - Use order queue – **becomes** Priority Scheduling

- Prepare in advance part of dishes that are the most ordered was **transformed** in an Urgent list that production send 1 to 2 days in advance with the most critical items in the production chain.

By the end, all the ideas from imaginary brainstorming were implemented in order to keep the same number of collaborators, delivering 140% more results than before the imaginary brainstorming.

2.4.6   Tricks and recommendations

The critical path

In the imaginary brainstorming, there are 2 critical steps in order to achieve good results: the definition of essential problem elements (step 3) and the transformation of ideas for the imaginary problem in suitable ideas for the real problem (step 7)

Take a suitable time for the imaginary ideas

Sometimes in the moment of transform one imaginary idea in real idea, it is hard to understand the correlation between both of them.

For that reason, spend a suitable amount of time trying to figure out how to connect the dots.

In general, I use a deadline of 5 minutes for idea so that I abandon the previous idea and move to other idea.

Enjoy the imagination

As the imaginary problem sometimes looks ridiculous, it is funny to imagine the ideas that we are proposing for real. This kind of energy and spirit stimulates the brain and makes people to open their minds to creativity

"When you make music or write or create, it's really your job to have mind-blowing, irresponsible, condomless sex with whatever idea it is you're writing about at the time. "

Lady Gaga

As a result of the explosion of knowledge which was generated during the last years. The development of new things sometime become restricted in several areas.

For that reason, the analogue method is so interesting to create new ideas based and mixed with other different ideas.

In general lines, this method consist in the Antoine Lavoisier famous quote:

> *"Nothing is lost, nothing is created, everything is transformed"*

Antoine Lavoisier

Therefore, this method is for whom love this concept!

The analogue method consists in the association and correlation analogue between several ideas in order to create something new.

2.5.1   Definition

The analogy method is a systematic method where the team members expand their ideas through the use of non-correlated figures, words, nature, patents and papers.

2.5.2   General overview

In this method, the team starts defining the problem by a structured brainstorming or brainwriting 6-3-5, where the ideas are exposed in front of all team members. Afterward, one analogue approach is defined (words, figure, images, nature, patents, combined, etc) in order to start the generation of analogue references.

Then, the team members apply ideas correlated to the analogue references to the problem.

In the next round the ideas are combined in order to generate new approaches of problem.

2.5.3   Applying the method

This method is most indicated **for midsize experienced teams (5 to 8 members)** where the members might have either **limited experience in creativity tools been**.

In this case, the **comprehension of the is not critical**, even though new approaches are needed.

Likewise, this tool is more recommended for **Understanding and Generation** stages of problem solving process.

Problems which required new alternative or new concepts or reconfiguration among specific domain or technology are the most common application of this tools. Therefore, it is possible to generate a controlled amount of ideas and concepts in a **very intermediate period of time.**

2.5.4   Step-By-Step

Step 1 – Define the goal or problem

Step 2 – Generate ideas by structured brainstorming or Brainwriting 6-3-5

Step 3 – Define type of analogue references (figures, images, nature, patents, combined, etc)

Step 4 – Collect analogue references

Step 5 – Select and discuss how to apply analogue references to the problem. Use only one analogue reference at time

Step 6 – Expose of the ideas generated by analogue correlation and combine them

Step 7 – Repeat the process as many time as necessary

2.5.5   Examples

Once our team were looking for innovative ways to create components for a laser cutting machine.

We were focused in reduce costs and simplify the manufacturing process.

In this case, we decided to use analogy creativity in order to get new ideas.

Then we started to list plenty of ideas from catalogues, Pinterest, benchmarking.

After brainstorming and brainwrinting sessions, we identified that laser cutting machine could produce flexible components, such as textiles. On the other hand, aligning shafts are difficult task and misalignments jeopardize machine movements . Because of that, self alignment bearing are used to solve such problems.

Therefore, in this small hobbyist project we decided to combine such amazing characteristics to produce self-alignment bearing in laser cutting wood ply.

Figure 11

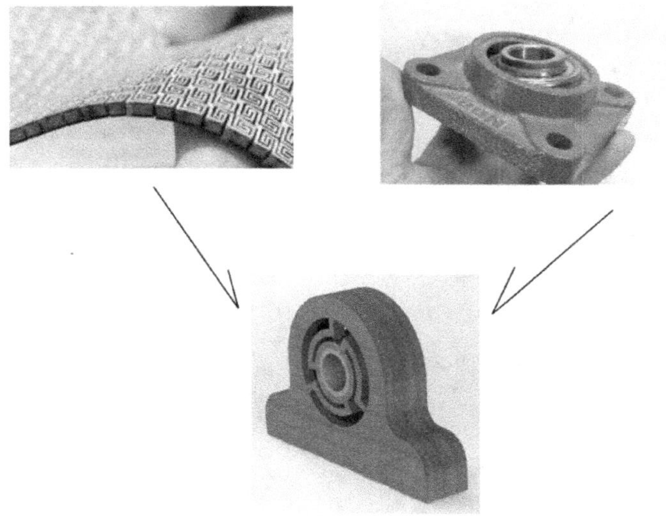

2.5.6 Tricks and recommendations (working pendent content)

Use Patent office's data base

Google Patents

WIPO

INPI
USPO

Use images database from apps and webpages

Pinterest

Google image

Pixabay

Use 3D model cloud

ThingIverse

3DHub

Grabcad

Myminifactory

Prusa

Be patient

"You can never solve a problem on the level on which it was created."

Albert Einstein

The morphological chart is one of the most systematic and structured creativity tools that is presented in this book.

In general lines, this method consist in explode the problem in small functions in order to define the problem morphology. As a consequence, main delivery of this method is a matrix chart where each row consist in a problem function while each column represent an option for the problem function.

Here is the secret of the morphological matrix. It is not the matrix which is important, but the combination between the options.

For example, a 8x5 morphological chart have potential to generate around 390 625 solutions.. If you compare this method with brainstorming where one idea is generate by minute, you will take 3 years to catch the same amount of ideas which the same 8x5 morphological chart can provide.

Figure 12

Solutions →

Problem Functions						
Function 1	Concept 1	Concept 2	Concept 3	Concept 4	Concept 5
Function 2	Concept 1	Concept 2	Concept 3	Concept 4	Concept 5
Function 3	Concept 1	Concept 2	Concept 3	Concept 4	Concept 5
Function 4	Concept 1	Concept 2	Concept 3	Concept 4	Concept 5
Function 5	Concept 1	Concept 2	Concept 3	Concept 4	Concept 5
Function 6	Concept 1	Concept 2	Concept 3	Concept 4	Concept 5
Function 7	Concept 1	Concept 2	Concept 3	Concept 4	Concept 5
Function 8	Concept 1	Concept 2	Concept 3	Concept 4	Concept 5

2.6.1 Definition

The morphological chart is a systematic creativity tool where practical solution are generated for a problem. In this case, the problem is exploded in problem functions or parameter. The focus of team member is the generation of ideas for the problem function so that a matrix is completed. Combining the solutions of each problem function the team can find a new solution for the problem.

2.6.2 General overview

In general, the morphological chart is an structured creativity method that help the creativity team to generate ideas based on the combination of solution options of each problem function.

This method can be used to reconfigurations, development of new products based on available technologies and brand new products. It is very popular for writers and designers that are looking for layout alternatives.

It is possible to use several other creativity tool combine with morphological chart, such as functional analysis (section 2.7), Brainstorming (section 2.2), brainwriting (section 2.3) , Pugh diagram (section 0), among others.

This method can be used with drawings, words and sketches/symbols, making the experience interesting to generate several ideas from the same combination of problem functions.

2.6.3   Applying the method

This method is most indicated **for midsize experienced teams (5 to 8 members)** where the members might have either **limited experience in creativity tools been.**

In this case, the **comprehension of the problem is significant**, even though new approaches are needed.

Likewise, this tool is more recommended for **Understanding and Generation** stages of problem solving process.

Problems which required new concepts or reconfiguration are the most common application of this tools. Therefore, it is possible to generate a controlled amount of ideas and concepts in a **medium or long period of time**.

2.6.4   Step-By-Step

Step 1 – Join team members and experts

Step 2 – Define problem functions or parameters for all possible solutions

Step 3 – List all the possible option for each problem function

Step 4 – Combine options and build alternative solutions

Step 5 – Analyze and select the most suitable alternative solution

2.6.5   Examples

In this example, we used morphological chart to generate ideas of mugs.

In this case, we identified 5 problem functions: Shape, Lid cap, opening, material and handle.

Therefore, the team member generated ideas for each function using brainstorming.

As the result, it was possible to identify a chart who was the basis for the idea generation.

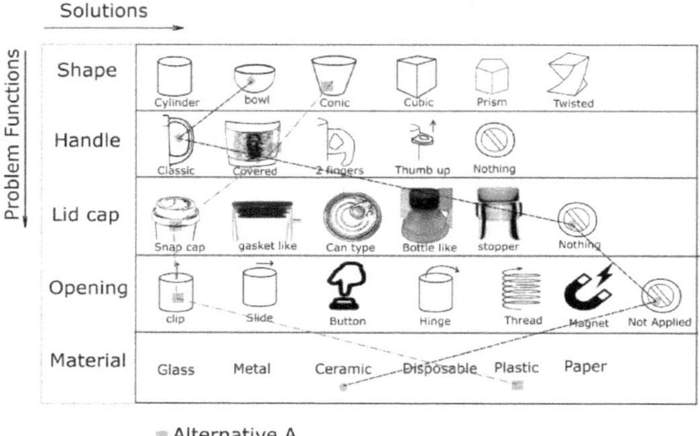

Therefore, from this point on, the team combined solutions in order to identify alternative ideas for the problem.

In this example, the figure presents 2 alternatives in accordance with the solution combination. But the total number of alternatives for this example is close to 6500 ideas . The best part is the fact that the creativity session took 20 minutes long to generate this chart.

Alternative A   Alternative B

2.6.6   Tricks and recommendations

Work with breaks

It high recommended to have short breaks during creativity sessions which applies morphological chart because of the big effort and abstraction involved in the process.

In this case, I recommend a short break between each problem function in order to turn the key in the team members mind.

Evaluate solutions quality

As the main goal of generation phase is to produce as many ideas as possible. Nevertheless, the morphological chart already brings this characteristic to us.

For that reason, it is important to generate ideas and options for each problem function which make sense for the problem. However, take care about this topic, otherwise the ideas and creativity will be restricted and blocked.

Create more than one idea from each alternative solution

Each combination of morphological chart can be used to generate more than one alternative solution.

Therefore, take time and develop new ideas upon the combination in order to create brand new ideas.

Transforming Trello in a Morphological Chart

One of the most useful online tool for agile management nowadays is Trello.

This tool can be used as a KANKAN which works collaboratively. For that reason, it is possible to create a morphological chart where the columns are the problem functions and each card describes the solution options for each function.

The next figure represents the same mug example in trello.

Figure 15

"You have to be burning with an idea, or a problem, or a wrong that you want to right. If you're not passionate enough from the start, you'll never stick it out."

Steve Jobs

Following the idea from heuristic redefinition, as well as morphological chart parametric analysis and other methods, the Functional analysis (or Function Structure of Function synthesis) main goal is to tear down a problem and split it in small subsystems.

In this case, there is a couple of really important things that functional analysis differs from other methods:

- Definition of systems and subsystems
- Correlation between systems
- Definition of energy, material and signal flow among systems

As a consequence, this type of structure allow us to identify the problem in several levels of abstractions in addition to analyze problems related to the interface between systems.

2.7.1   Definition

The Functional Analysis is a problem solving method that consists in the conversion of problem in subsystems which is correlated by the flow of energy, signal and material.

2.7.2   General overview

The functional structure is a method based on subsystems and flow of energy, signal and material.

The systems and flow are described in a flow diagram where:

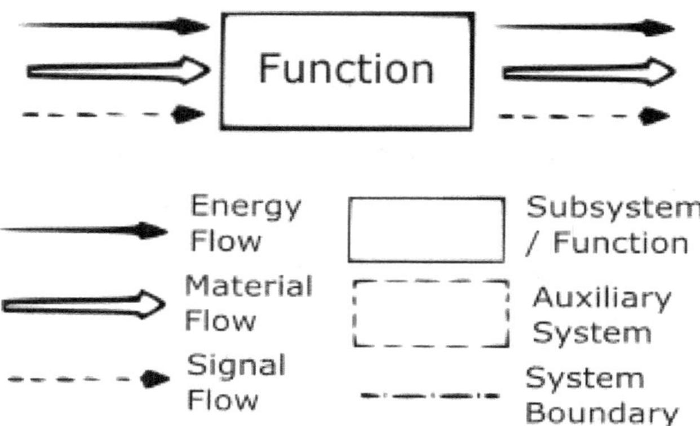

Therefore, it is possible to establish different levels of abstraction for the problem whereas the global function is the most basic definition of the problem. In this case, each function can be detailed and split in other subfunctions.

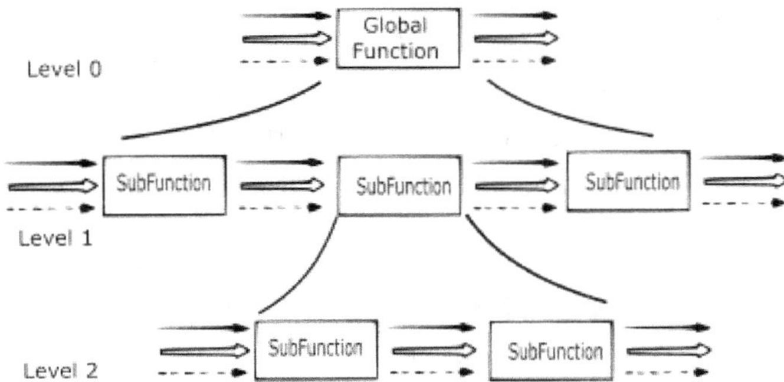

Therefore, any other creativity method can be used in each flow or system in order to identify new solution which will modify the overall (global) system.

One example of a first level of abstraction is presented bellow. This example describes the global function of a universal testing machine, which is used to identify the strength of a product, material r component.

Figure 18

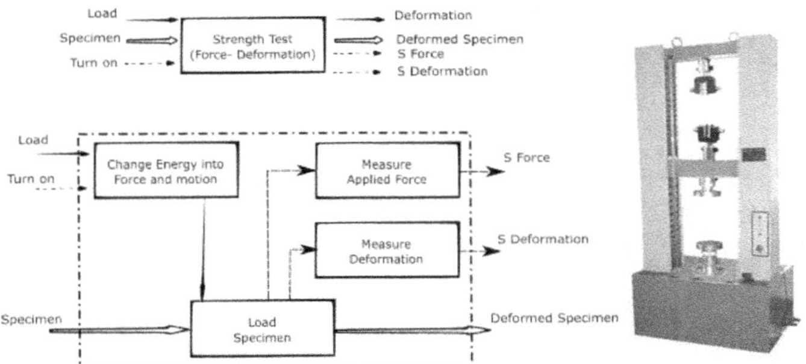

It is also very common to treat the global function as a BlackBox where a group of thing enter in one side and go out the desired delivery on the other side.

In order to increase the level of abstraction, several authors indicate a group of magical words to be used to represent any function in product design. The basic 5 words and their opposite are:

- Change / Keep
- Vary / return
- Connect / disconnect
- Channel / not channel
- Store / Release

On the other hand, those words can be detailed and standardized by 12 generalized words:

Figure 19

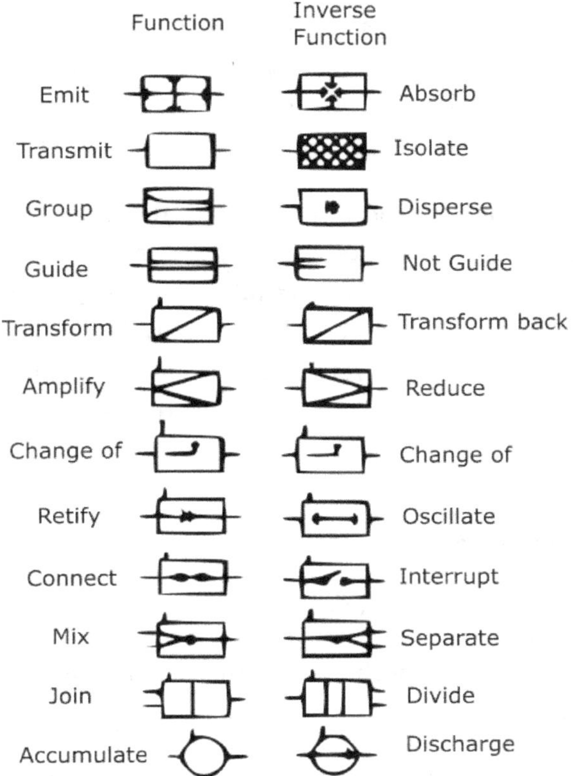

2.7.3 Applying the method

This method is most indicated **for midsize experienced teams (5 to 8 members)** where the members might have either **wide experience in creativity tools been.**

In this case, the **comprehension of the problem is either limited or wide**, even though new approaches are needed.

Likewise, this tool is more recommended for **Establishing and Understanding** stages of problem solving process. This method is a wonderful tool to be used with Morphological Charts.

Problems which required new alternative or new concepts or reconfiguration among specific domain or technology among current available knowledge are the most common application of this tools. Therefore, it is possible to generate new perspectives and understanding of a problem **in a small period of time**.

2.7.4   Step-By-Step

Step 1 – Join team members and experts

Step 2 – Define the problem and the overall function (global Function)

Step 3 – Explode the global function in subfunctions

Step 4 – Define signal, energy and material functions flow

Step 5 – Create Functions boundary

Step 6 – Use other creativity tool do find solutions for each function and their interfaces, such as Brainstorming, Morphological Charts, among others

2.7.5   Examples

It is interesting to note that any project, problem and opportunity can be exploded in small subfunctions.

In the first time I used Functional analysis in combination with benchmarking techniques, I was part of a product development team which was in charge of the creation of an innovative solution in white goods and appliances. As result of the first mapping of the potential problem to solve, it was possible to divide experts in squads.

In this example, I will show you how it is possible to extract the functional structure from an existent product and transform it completely.

The product which we will exemplify this method is a scale for coffee brewers.

In general lines, the main function of scale is to weight the amount of coffee grains/powder and poured water in the coffee moisture.

As a consequence, it is possible to prepare coffee with repeatability and with different intensities, aroma and acidity as a function of the amount of water, coffee, size of grain and water temperature.

Most of scales for coffee making has some features in order to attend baristas needs:

- Measurement of mass (weight)
- Timer
- Tare
- Auto-off

Figure 20

After join a group of experts in coffee making, electronics, design and product engineering (**Step 1**), it was possible to **define the problem and the overall function (global Function) as indicated in the method Step 2.**

In this case, we identified that the overall function was:

"Measure coffee and water as a function of time "

Figure 21

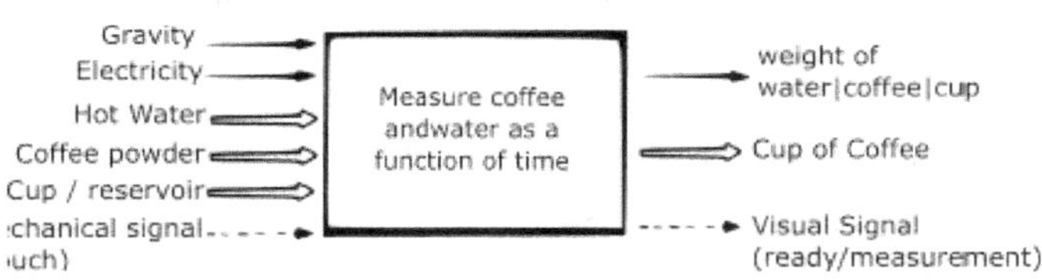

In the sequence, we defined de 1st level of structure abstraction, where the subfunctions are extracted from the overall function (**Step 3**).

In the first round, we identified 8 subfunctions:

- Support cup/reservoir
- Control Equipment
- Measurement
- Register
- Tare
- Timer
- Show Results/Instructions
- Guide User

Afterwards, it was possible to identify the interaction between function caused by signal, energy and material flow (**Step 4**).

In this case, Electricity and gravity are the energy which make the measurement function to work. In addition, electricity is also used to control the equipment and showing results and instructions.

The cup, coffee powder and hot water are the material which enter into the system, while the cup of coffee is delivered.

Inside the subsystem, the mechanical signal (touch) activates control equipment function which send the signal to measurement unity, guide user and show results functions.

Figure 22

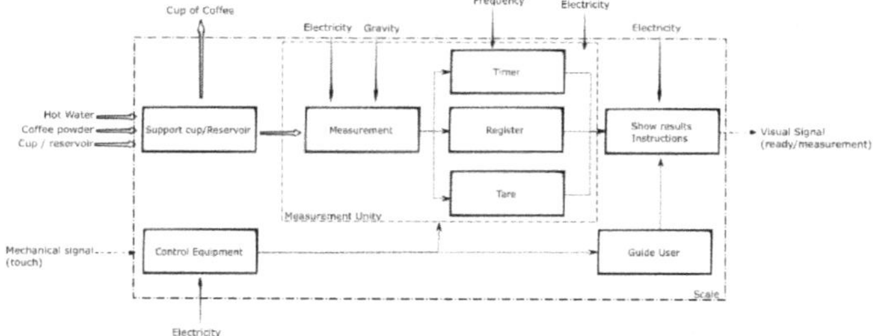

Using a fast change of the functions: Control Equipment, guide user and show results; It was possible to create a new smart product based in mobile and IoT technology.

The Acaia company had exactly this idea. They decided that the signal from the show results and control equipment function to be performed by the a mobile App. In this case, the guide user function instruct the user about the brew history and their preferences.

Figure 23

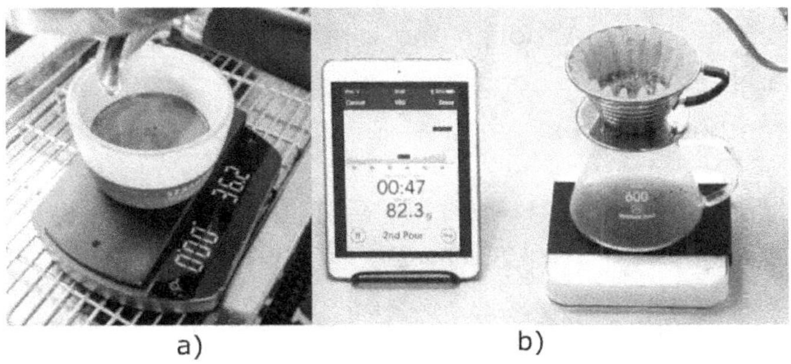

a)   b)

2.7.6   Tricks and recommendations

Start small – It is common that creativity and development teams increase the complexity of the process in order to understand thing in detail. In this method, try start with baby steps, increasing the complexity of the subfunction one level at time.

Just increase the number of subfunctions if it is absolutely necessary.

Use the standardize words – As presented in this section, there are several standardized words to describe functions. These words are complementary and help you to describe functions in a extremely generic way.

Be flexible – Although the method has several steps and elements, don't feel obligated to use all the method features.

Use what is necessary, For example, energy and signal function flow are not necessary in most of cases.

Therefore, try to image this method as blackboxes where something enter and get out transformed.

"If you're not prepared to be wrong, you'll never come up with anything original."

Ken Robinson

The Parametric analysis is another creativity tool that helps you to identify the key improvement aspects in comparison with an existent solution.

In this case, this method is very usual in benchmarking and teardown analyses because it is possible to evaluate the main differences, advantages and disadvantages of each solution in order to combine, improve and even identify point that will require further interactions.

2.8.1   Definition

The idea of parametric analysis is based on establishing parameters and variables. These parameter might be qualitative or quantitative, being possible to address weight for each parameter.

2.8.2   General overview

This method consists in the comparison between existent solutions in order to catch the best aspects of all the competitors and combine in new alternatives.

In general lines, the parametric analysis is an powerful tool to fast incremental results where the main goal is to overcome the competitors and generate small differentiation in the market.

This method is usually applied combined with benchmarking and teardown methods where the products or solution from the competitors are dissected in order to understand and learn the mistakes and successes of competition.

By the end, it is possible to create new solutions with combine successes of competitors.

2.8.3   Applying the method

This method is most indicated **for midsize experienced teams (5 to 8 members)** where the members might have **wide experience in creativity tools been.**

In this case, the **comprehension of the problem is well-known,** even though new approaches are needed.

Likewise, this tool is more recommended for **Understanding and Generation** stages of problem solving process.

Problems which required reconfiguration and new approaches among specific domain or technology are the most common application of this tools. Therefore, it is possible to generate a controlled amount of ideas and concepts in a **very small period of time.**

2.8.4   Step-By-Step

Step 1 – Join team members and experts

Step 2 – Define the analysis parameters or variables and weights

Step 3 – List all the main competitors, current solutions or reference solution to be improved

Step 4 – Collect data and fulfill the parametric analysis table

Step 5 – Generate solution combining the strongest parameters of all analyzed competitors

Step 6 – Generate ideas to overcome the strongest parameters of competitors (prioritize the parameters that are the most important for your customer)

Bonus step – Generate ideas that add 3 new parameters that only your solution will address

2.8.5 Examples

About 13 years ago, one customer approached me asking to innovate his product. He had found me because of 3D printing services which he associated with innovation. In matter of fact, he was luckily right because our company developed innovative products .

Then, he presented his product : a wire clothes hanger.

In this case, we start facing one of the most common products in the market and we decided to perform several creativity sessions as a part of product development process.

In this example, we used parametric analysis in order to generate ideas for differentiate product in the market.

Step 2 Therefore, we defined the most common parameters as:

- Price:
- Material :
- Maximum load :
- Size :
- Color :
- Rubber cover:
- Pants support
- Shirt support
- Support for delicate women shirt

Step 3 and 4 In addition, we selected the top 3 competitors in order to analyze fulfill the parametric table.

Figure 24

Price:	2	1	4
Material :	wood	plastic	Metal
Maximum load :	15kg	5kg	1 kg/hang
Size :	medium	medium	big
Color :	yellow	black	White
Rubber cover:	no	no	no
Pants support	yes	yes	no
Shirt support	yes	yes	yes
Support for delicate women shirt	yes	no	no

Step 5 - Analyzing this table, we identified the strongest and weakest points of all competitors. And combined in order to create new solutions.

Figure 25

	Concept 1
Price:	2
Material :	Plastic
Maximum load :	15kg
Size :	Small / Retract
Color :	color
Rubber cover:	yes
Pants support	yes
Shirt support	yes
Support for delicate women shirt	yes

By the end, we decided to go further and create a new parameters which no competitor has. We create a brand new parameter, the ability of fold (whether or not the hanger was foldable).

As a consequence, we identified more than 3 ideas, where the follow figure indicates the prototype photo one of them .

Figure 26

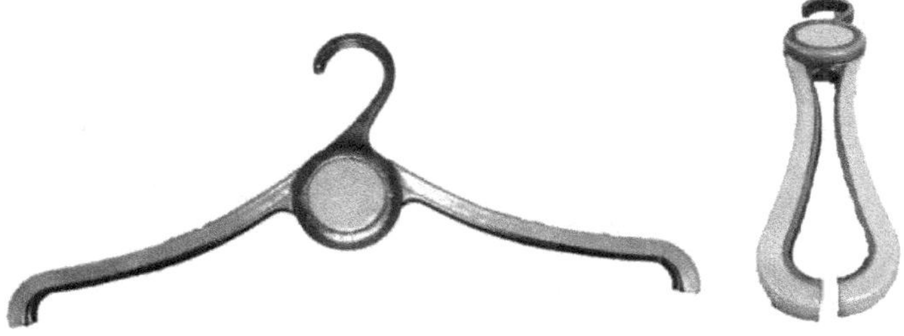

2.8.6   Tricks and recommendations

Use parameters where it is possible to compare

In most of cases where parametric analysis is used , it is possible to acquire data from datasheet and manuals . For that reason, don't waste time inventing parameters to compare. Use exactly the same parameters of competitors specification in order to kick-off the analysis

Create new parameters in order to increase perceived value

On approach to differentiate your product from the competitors is to create a new specification, parameter or feature for the product.

In The Blue Ocean Strategy, this approach is applied in the valuable curve in order to establish a new market.

"Creativity, as has been said, consists largely of rearranging what we know in order to find out what we do not know. Hence, to think creatively, we must be able to look afresh at what we normally take for granted." George Kneller

In this method, the main goal is to correlate market/customers and products parameters in order to identify opportunities and understand the problem matter.

The product-market matrix (Ansoff matrix) is an excellent method to help you to understand what you are proposing and delivering.

2.9.1   Definition

The Product-Market matrix is a creativity method that consistently correlates the information of existing and products parameters against existing and new markets/customers.

2.9.2   General overview

In general lines, this method looks like an expanded parameters analysis where the team member looks for ideas of marketing/customer, and new products/services.

The structure of the matrix consists in 4 quadrants in accordance with the market strategy: Market penetration; Market Development; Product Development and Diversification.

Figure 27

		Products	
		Current	New
Market	Current	Market Penetration	Product Development
	New	Market Development	Diversification

2.9.3 Applying the method

This method is most indicated **for midsize experienced teams (3 to 5 members)** where the members might have either **wide experience in creativity tools been.**

In this case, the **comprehension of the problem is wide**, even though new approaches are needed.

Likewise, this tool is more recommended for **Establish and Understanding** stages of problem solving process.

Problems which required new alternative or new concepts or reconfiguration among specific domain or technology are the most common application of this tools for difficult decision making and problem understanding.

2.9.4   Step-By-Step

Step 1 – Join team members and experts

Step 2 – Define the analysis parameters or variables and weights

Step 3 – List all the main competitors, current solutions or reference solution to be improved

Step 4 – List all the main market or customers for current solutions or reference solution to be improved

Step 5 – Use any other creativity tool, such as brainstorming or brainwriting, in order to identify new market segments

Step 6 – Use any other creativity tool, such as parametric analysis and brainstorming, in order to identify new products parameters

Step 7 – Identify the size of market and competiveness level of each product parameter and market segment/ customer

Step 8 – Generate solution combining the strongest parameters of all analyzed competitors

Step 9 – Identify where are the gaps of marketing or which segment is poorly supported

Step 10 – Define the problem and goal in accordance with the strategy: Market penetration, Product development, product diversification, or market development

2.9.5   Examples

Once, I had a customer who was as passionate about coffee as I am. He looked for me intrigued about a new product and how he could create a revolution in coffee brew.

Therefore, after understand the general ideas and market, we decided to apply Product-Market Matrix in order to analyze how the product and market strategy should be.

Step 1 – I have a couple of meetings with remarkable baristas and also with home brewers in order to identify main characteristics and parameters which I could use in the analysis.

Step 2 –In this example, I will simplify and just use the main parameters in order to illustrate the method.

- Product Size
- Capacity Liters (Oz)
- Aesthetic
- Speed

- Power
- Capsule feature
- Filter feature
- Espresso feature
- Automatic Water heat
- Automatic preparation
- Portable
- Cost

Step 3 – In the next step, we identify the main players in accordance with the type of coffee maker in order to analyze a general perspective. In other cases we select exactly the competitors and products.

As result, we identified:

- Mr Coffee Like – drip coffee
- Low Espresso maker
- Professional Espresso Machine
- Nespresso like – Capsule/pad based
- French Press like –
- Aeropress Like -
- Manual Filtered –
- Portable coffee maker

Step 4 – Amazingly, the previous step of this method had already started to stimulate new ideas and new markets, even though it was not finished.

Take care about this feeling, and don't jump steps before finish the method. It worthwhile!

Considering this stage of the method, we identified several customer profiles in order to create a classification of this market. As a simplified result, I can list:

- Home Brewers at home
- Professional Brewers
- Coffee Nerds
- Coffee to Go Customers
- Travelers
- Camping and hiking
- Students
- Coffee house customers

Step 5 – Using a classical structured, we identify new market/customers segments with combined previous markets/customers:

- Personalized coffee for coffee nerds
- High quality coffee to go
- Coffee everywhere for Adventure customers
- Affordable Coffee on demand

Step 6 – Following the same idea, we also identified new products parameters in order to attend current and new customers demands.

In this stage, it is recommended to create at least 3 new parameters.

Therefore, it was found:

- Connectivity
- Battery Autonomy
- Automatic coffee Intensity
- Register of Customer preferences

You have been imaging that just these stages were already unbelievable . That is right, it is indeed. But wait for the next stages.

Step 7 – After collecting all this data and generating new ideas for market, customers and product/service parameters, it is time to evaluate market size and competiveness level of each product parameter and market segments.

As a result, it was possible to identify opportunities in Product development strategy, as well as diversification. In addition, A new product parameters was also identified: The Mug Coffee Maker which is connected with your mobile in order to identify your profile of coffee intensity. In this case, the mug is

compounded by both pad and capsules where no cab e
is needed to work, as it is battery powered.

Figure 28

Legend:
- Clear Leader ●
- One of Leader ◕
- Follower ◑
- Minor Player ◔
- No presence ○

Market		Type of Products — Current								Type of Products — New
		Mr Coffee Like drip coffee	Espresso maker	Professional Espresso	Nespresso like Capsule/pad based	French Press like	Aeropress Like -	Manual Filtered –	Portable coffee maker	Mug Coffee Maker (Automatic coffee, Intensity, Connectivity, Register of Customer preferences, Battery Autonomy)
Current	Home Brewers at home	●	◔	○	◕	◔	◔	◑	○	
	Professional Brewers	○	◕	●	◕	◕	◔	◕	○	
	Coffee Nerds	◔	◕	●	◔	◑	◕	◔	○	Opportunity
	Coffee to Go Customers	●	◕	○	◔	○	○	○	○	Opportunity
	Travelers	○	○	○	○	◑	●	◑	◔	Opportunity
	Camping and hiking	◔	○	○	◔	◑	●	◕	◕	Opportunity
	Students	◑	◕	○	◔	◔	○	●	○	Opportunity
	Coffee house customers	○	◕	●	◔	◑	◑	◕	○	
New	Personalized coffee for coffee nerds	○	◕	◕	◕	◕	◕	◕	○	Opportunity
	High quality coffee to go	◔	◕	◕	◕	○	○	○	○	Opportunity
	Coffee everywhere for Adventure customers	○	○	○	○	○	◔	◔	◔	Opportunity
	Affordable Coffee on demand	◔	○	○	○	◑	◕	◕	◔	Opportunity

2.9.6 Tricks and recommendations

Use PEST(PESTLE/PESTEL, PESTLIED, STEEPLE, SLEPT, LONGPESTLE) Analysis for evaluate correlation between current products and markets. All these mnemonics represent different dimensions of social, economical and technological characteristics which surround business and creativity.

- **PESTLE/PESTEL:** Political, Economic, Socio-Cultural, Technological, Legal, Environmental.
- **PESTLIED**: Political, Economic, Socio-Cultural, Technological, Legal, International, Environmental, Demographic.
- **STEEPLE**: Social/Demographic, Technological, Economic, Environmental, Political, Legal, Ethical.
- **SLEPT**: Socio-Cultural, Legal, Economic, Political, Technological.
- **LONGPESTLE**: Local, National, and Global versions of PESTLE. (These are best used for understanding change in multinational organizations.)

Use SWOT (Strengths, Weaknesses, Opportunities and Threats) analysis for evaluate new markets

Target different geographical markets at home or abroad.

Conduct a PEST Analysis or use the **CAGE Distance Framework** to identify opportunities and threats in this different market.

Use different sales channels, such as online or direct sales, if you are currently selling through agents or intermediaries.

Use Market Segmentation to target different groups of people, perhaps with different age, gender or demographic profiles from your usual customers.

Use the marketing mix to understand how to reposition your product.

"To live a creative life, we must lose our fear of being wrong."
Clinton Chilton Pearce

The C-K Theory is a creativity model where the knowledge domain (K) and the concept domain(C) are confronted side-by-side.

In this method, it is possible to identify the fundamental knowledge and technologies which a concept requires to be implemented.

2.10.1 Definition

By definition, the C-K theory is the method where the creativity concepts and technical knowledge are graphically disposed in a mind mapping side-by-side. Therefore, it is possible to identify knowledge gaps to be developed in addition to organize the current available knowledge to implement concepts.

In this method, the concepts (C-Space) is expected to propose ideas with no pre-existing status in K-Space, while the Knowledge ideas (K-Space) focus in identifying solutions based on existent knowledge.

2.10.2 General overview

In general lines, the C-K Theory consists in the systematic development of Concepts and research of state of art (knowledge basis).

Well, Although C-K theory is a systematic method, there is no recipe about how to start the analysis.

Therefore, I will show you what several researchers and I adopted.

We start from the K-Space, investigating the current knowledge, state of art, patents and legacy.

Each round of creativity session we change from one space to other. In addition, we also adopt an extra round only to identify correlations between C and K spaces.

Those correlations are called C-K operators, where the correlation between knowledge to concept is called Disjunction. In this case, the current knowledge can be used to develop and implement the concept.

Figure 29

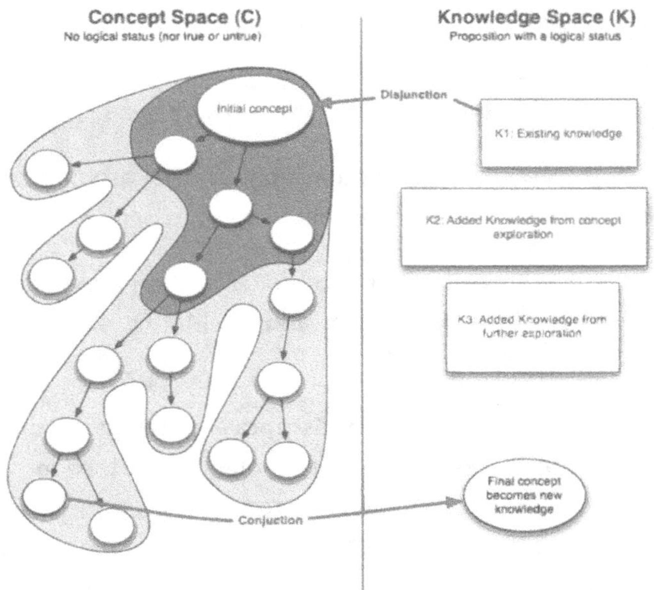

On the other hand, the correlation between concept to knowledge is called Conjunction. In this case, the concept don't have previous knowledge basis implying on development of new technology or knowledge.

By the end, the use of one concept to generate another concept is called idea expansion. It can also be applied to knowledge which is used to develop new knowledge.

2.10.3 Applying the method

This method is most indicated **for midsize experienced teams (5 to 8 members)** where the members might have either **wide experience in creativity tools been**.

In this case, the **comprehension of the problem is limited**, even though new approaches are needed.

Likewise, this tool is more recommended for **Understanding, Generation and Evaluating** stages of problem solving process.

Problems which required disruptive concepts among specific/new domain or technology are the most common application of this tools. Therefore, it is possible to generate a controlled amount of ideas and concepts and knowledge in a **mid-term development** .

2.10.4 Step-By-Step

Step 1 – Join team members and experts

Step 2 – Define the problem

Step 3 – List all the solutions to solve the problem in the current knowledge (K-space)

Step 4 – Create concepts (C-space) which explore either new ideas which is mix current knowledge or ideas which is not found in K-Space

Step 5 – Use any other creativity tool, such as brainstorming or brainwriting, in order to identify possible correlation between C and K spaces

Step 6 – Identify the concepts which requires development of new knowledge

Step 7 – Develop researches which expand the current knowledge and support the concepts

Step 8 – Expand the concepts from C-Space generating new idea branches

Step 9- Repeat the process until identifying feasible solutions

2.10.5 Examples

In this example, I will tell you the story of 3M Post-it. In this development, 3M were not looking for such a product.

They were looking for new super strong glue for the industrial branch of company. Nevertheless, they found this soft and reusable glue, which was applied in the Post-it products.

It is important to note that they did not use C-K theory, because they discovered this product by accident. But, the logic in this example will help you to understand the working principle of C-K Theory.

Many other companies uses C-K theory to develop their products and innovative technologies, such as

But let's continue with the example of Post-it.

At the beginning, the main idea was to find a super strong glue (**Step 2**)

Step 3- In the K-Space, it was listed most of knowledge related to glue development, such as glue chemistry, polymers, Rheology, et cetera.

Step 4 – Therefore, several concepts were developed based on the existent knowledge, resulting in one peculiar concept: soft glue.

Step 5 – Using creativity tools, several ideas were identified to use such a soft glue. As a result, it was found that **soft glue** might **be used for marking**.

Step 6 – In order to make this concept possible, it was also identified new knowledge that need to be developed. In this case, several other ideas were involved, such as type of paper, selling strategy and how to use it.

Step 7 – the idea expanded in a way that it was separated from the initial problem in order to be detailed and become a new product.

Step 6 – As this idea expanded and create its own development body. It was possible to expand the concepts from C-Space generating new idea branches, such as book page markers , different sizes, colors and applications for this new product.

Figure 30

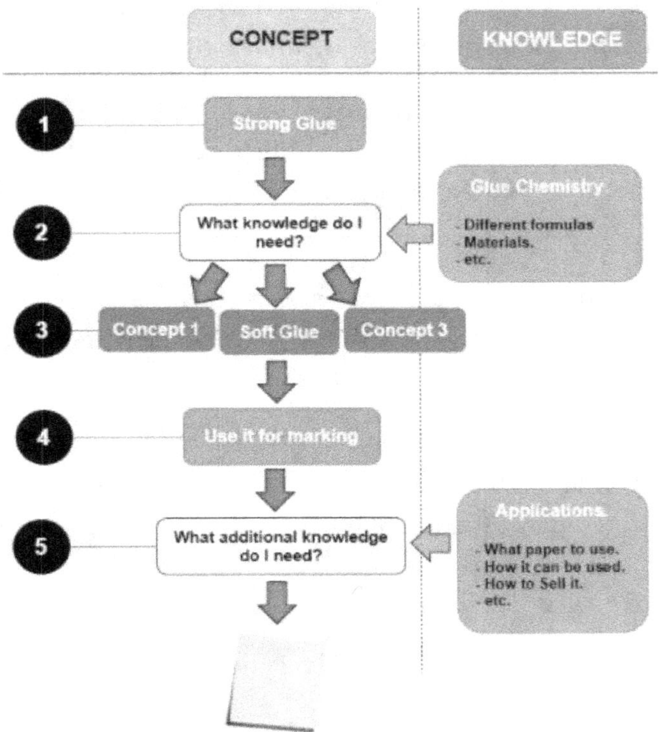

2.10.6 Tricks and recommendations

Periodicity is the key for the success

This method is a quite time consuming in comparison with other methods which I presented to you in this book.

Nevertheless, it is also the method that aim to reach the most disruptive innovations as well.

Therefore, it is important to allocate suitable amount of time in order to succeed. Another point in is the fact that this method is very strategic and focused in long term results .

This method looks like a marathon, not a sprint. For that reason, it is important that all team members develop the habit to spend time in the project in the daily basis.

In addition, the team leader need to ensure the focus of group in periodic creativity sessions, such as weekly meetings.

Don't lose focus

As this method is focused in long-term results, it is very common to identify plenty of branches and opportunities.

That is a trap in several levels, whereas people got more involved with the problem branches than with the actual problem that they are solving.

In order to avoid to fall in such a trap, several researchers recommend to have 2-3 iterations of investigation for each branch.

Register braches out of scope

On the other hand, branches that go out of scope might still create very good opportunities. For that reason, all branches that were discarded by the iteration threshold need to be documented in order to be reviewed in a future moment.

"Creativity is God's gift to us. Using our creativity is our gift back to God."

Julia Cameron

Another fantastic creativity tool is called SCAMPER, which is the acronym for actions that force you to think outside the box.

This method is extremely easy because it was developed to lead your ideas in accordance with different applications.

For example, it is possible to **P**ut another use (scam **P** er) to a simple Cup and transform it in a Pen Holder.

2.11.1 General overview

In general lines, the SCAMPER is a method that consists in a iterative cycle compounded by 7 strategies or Actions.

In this method, the meaning of SCAMPER derivates from:

- **S**ubstitute
- **C**ombine
- **A**dapt

- **M**odify
- **P**ut to another use
- **E**liminate
- **R**everse

This acronym also has alternative interpretations according to the language and number of actions. For example, it this method is commonly found as **MESCRAI**.

- **M**odify
- **E**liminate
- **S**ubstitute
- **C**ombine
- **R**earrange
- **A**dapt
- **I**nvert

Another approach for this method is also found as **SCAMCEA**:

- **S**ubstitute
- **C**ombine
- **A**dapt/amplify
- **M**odify
- **C**ollocate with another use
- **E**liminate
- **A**rrange

Apart from the acronym which is used, the SCAMPER cycle consists in the sequence of creativity goals which leads the identification of different approaches for the same problem.

Figure 31

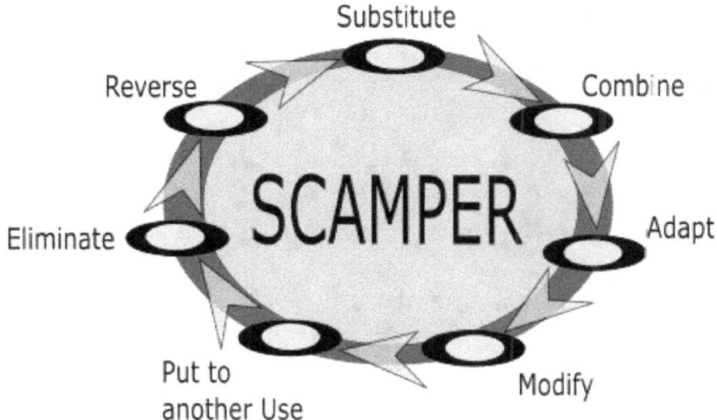

2.11.2 Applying the method

This method is most indicated **for small non-experienced teams (2 to 3 members)** where the members might have either **limited experience in creativity tools been**.

In this case, the **comprehension of the problem is intermediate**, even though new approaches are needed.

Likewise, this tool is more recommended for **Generation** stage of problem solving process.

Problems which required new alternative or new concepts or reconfiguration among specific domain or technology are the most common application of this tools. Therefore, it is possible to generate a controlled amount of ideas and concepts in a **very small period of time**.

2.11.3 Step-By-Step

Step 1 – Join team members

Step 2 – Define the problem

Step 3 – Use some **creativity tool**, such as Brainstorming, for generate Ideas related to how to **Substitute** things, functions or components to solve the problem.

Step 4 – Use some **creativity tool**, such as Brainstorming, for generate Ideas related to how to **Combine** things, functions or components to solve the problem..

Step 5 – Use some **creativity tool**, such as Brainstorming, for generate Ideas related to how to

Adapt things, functions or components to solve the problem..

Step 6 – Use some **creativity tool**, such as Brainstorming, for generate Ideas related to how to **Modify** things, functions or components to solve the problem.

Step 7 – Use some **creativity tool**, such as Brainstorming, for generate Ideas related to how to **Put another use to** things, functions or components to solve the problem.

Step 8 – Use some **creativity tool**, such as Brainstorming, for generate Ideas related to how to **Eliminate** things, functions or components to solve the problem.

Step 7- Use some **creativity tool**, such as Brainstorming, for generate Ideas related to how to **Reverse** things, functions or components to solve the problem.

Step 8 – Validate ideas and repeat the process

2.11.4 Examples

Once, our team has been hired to create new alternatives for a new product where a looker was needed.

In this first concept, the general idea was to use the looker lever to unlock the mechanism which would open the door. In this concept, the button was compounded by 3 components. Although the concept solve the problem, it still lacked of innovative characteristics and aesthetic appeal.

Therefore, our team decided to use SCAMPER method to identify different alternatives for the actuator button.

Figure 32

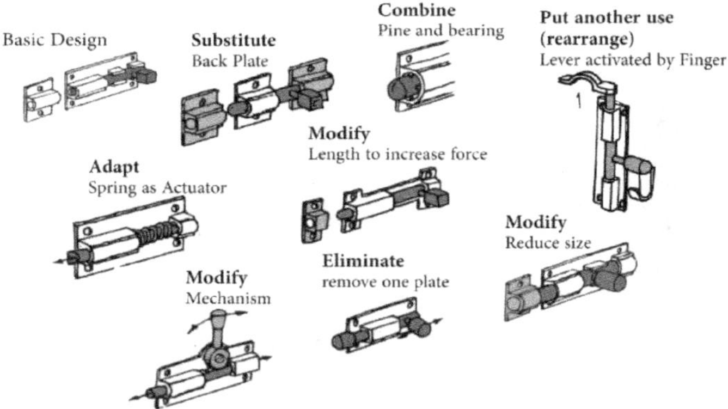

2.11.5 Tricks and recommendations

Be careful about complex products

It is important to note that scamper is a method developed for subsystems and simple products.

If you use in very complex products, sometimes each modifier will bring almost no difference for the overall product.

For example, applying Substitute Function in a CNC machine might imply on replacing Bearing or any other mechanical component. In addition, substituting LCD HIM (Human interface module) for a OLED HIM. That improve almost nothing in the perceived value of product.

Therefore, use it wisely in small simple systems that might improve value from the point of view of customer perception.

Define limit of iterations

Most of times perfectionist people tend to continuing using scamper cycles over and over again in order to fine new and more innovative solutions.

It is important to note that a limit of iteration is a balanced point where you can achieve innovative and creative alternatives in addition to attending the basic needs and specifications of your customer.

Remember, quality is what your customer see, therefore.

My suggestion is to use scamper in 3 cycles in order to obtain 3 ideas for each alternative. In this way, you will obtain around 512 alternative.

Use concept selection tools

As the scamper help you to generate plenty of ideas, it is important to use a convergent creativity method such as concept selection tools in order to funnel the ideas and identify the most suitable to implement in your design.

Next chapter will bring you the most powerful tool for concept selection and I strongly recommend you to learn and implement each one in order to identify the most interesting tool in accordance with your needs and expertise.

"The thing about creativity is, people are going to laugh at it. Get over it."

Twyla Tharp

3 Concept Selection and Decision Making

In the nominal group technique, the process of selecting an idea or concept is based on the minimal human interaction.

In general lines, this method consists in a poll where each team member vote and rank the ideas descendant from the best idea until the poorest idea.

It is an interesting approach for team which have not a wide experience working together besides avoiding conflicts.

3.1.1 Definition

The nominal group technique is a selection tool which consists in anonymous voting process.

3.1.2 General overview

In general lines, the nominal group technique starts from the ideas organization in post-its in a board. After organizing the ideas to be evaluated, each member w ll create a voting card (post-it) where all the ideas will be ranked from the best to the worst idea.

After the voting stage, all the cards were collected and analyzed in a way that each idea receive a total score (sum of all cards ranking position).

By the end, the total score will indicate which idea is the most suitable to go the next step of development.

3.1.3   Applying the method

This method is most indicated **for midsize experienced teams (5 to 8 members)** where the members might have either **limited experience in creativity tools been**.

In this case, the **comprehension of the problem is limited**, even though new approaches are needed.

Likewise, this tool is more recommended for **Evaluation and definition** stages of problem solving process.

Problems which required convergence of ideas and concepts in addition to decision making are the most common application of this tools. Therefore, it is possible to converge a wide number of ideas and concepts in a **very small period of time**, with **no resources** and **no conflicts**.

3.1.4   Step-By-Step

Step 1 – Join team members

Step 2 – List all the ideas and concepts generated previously

Step 3 – Organize ideas in a whiteboard or flipchart addressing a letter for each concept/idea

Step 4 – Eliminate redundancies and clarify ideas

Step 5 – Each team member ranks the ideas from the best to worst idea. In this case, the worst idea is 1 and the best idea is the number of ideas to be evaluated. For example, if you are analyzing 10 ideas, the best idea will be 10, and the worst idea will be 1.

Step 6 – Combine ranking and identify the total score

Step 7 – Deliberate the final ideas ranking

3.1.5   Examples

This method is extremely simple and the benefits of it is giant. It is excellent for whom that have decide or select a concept among a group of concepts which are majorly qualitative. In these cases, the opinions are the most important aspects in the decision.

It is very interesting to note that once our company was developing new textures for a product surface. At that moment, there was no technical specification that would indicate us a favorite.

For that reason, we decided to apply a fast nominal group technique to select the most suitable surface textures for our design.

We had 10 textures to evaluate and 8 team members

Figure 33

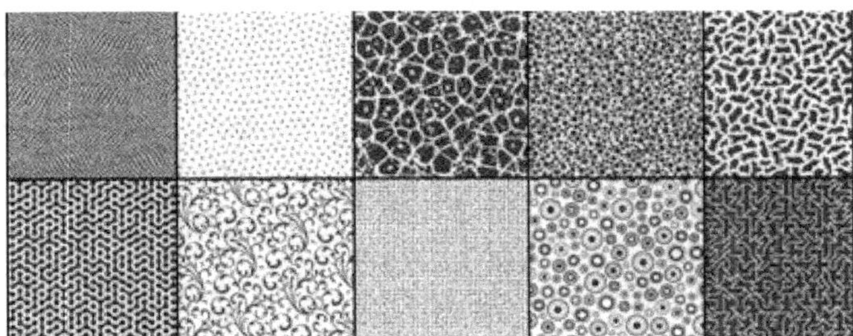

After the voting process, we combined the rankings and identified that the most suitable texture for our project would be the Texture 7.

Figure 34

Team member	Texture 1	Texture 2	Texture 3	Texture 4	Texture 5	Texture 6	Texture 7	Texture 8	Texture 9	Texture 10
john	1	7	3	2	6	4	8	10	9	5
Marlon	3	5	4	1	2	6	7	10	5	9
Mark	7	3	2	6	4	8	10	9	5	1
Joe	5	4	1	2	6	7	10	5	3	9
Mary	10	1	7	3	2	6	4	8	9	5
Jennifer	8	10	9	5	1	7	3	2	6	4
Richard	7	10	5	3	9	5	4	1	2	6
Patrick	1	7	3	2	6	4	9	5	8	10
Total score	42	47	34	24	36	47	55	50	47	49
Ranking	7	4	9	10	8	4	1	2	4	3

3.1.6 Tricks and recommendations

Use electronic poll

Nowadays, it is very interesting to use electronic poll in order to analyze the results and make a decision. In this case, I suggest a couple of tools that are very interesting:

- Google meeting – Poll
- Trello poll
- Slack poll
- Chat poll (any chat is good enough, such as whatsapp, wechat, skype, among others)

Using nominal group technique in Google Sheet

Another different approach is to used collaborative tools as a digital board where it is possible to apply the nominal group technique.

In this context, I suggest you to start using **Google Sheets**, whereas it is a very known and well established tool which almost everyone in the planet has access.

"Make an empty space in any corner of your mind, and creativity will instantly fill it."

Dee Hock

Another tool for concepts selection and decision making is the Pugh diagram. This method is also called relative decision chart because all the analysis are based in a reference concept.

In general lines this method compares each concept against the reference concept in order to identify whether the functions, specifications or characteristics are better, equal or worse than the reference.

3.2.1   Definition

By definition, the Pugh diagram is a correlation chart that compares functions/criteria/parameters and concepts with respect to a reference point (concept) .

This type of method is an analytical method to compare a large number of concepts and parameters in a per-to-per analysis.

3.2.2   General overview

The **Pugh diagram** consists in a **correlation chart** where the first column indicates the **qualitative or quantitative** characteristics to evaluate the concepts.

On the other hand all the concepts to be evaluated are listed in the first line of the chart.

Figure 35

Selection criteria	Reference Concept	Concept A	Concept B	Concept C	Concept D
Criterion 1	0	-	+	+	0
Criterion 2	0	+	+	0	0
Criterion 3	0	+	+	+	-
Criterion 4	0	0	0	+	-
Criterion 5	0	0	-	-	+
Total (+)	0	2	3	3	1
Total (-)	0	1	1	1	2
Total (0)	5	2	1	1	2
Net Score	0	1	2	2	-1
Decision	No	Consider	Consider	Consider	No

After selecting one concept as reference, we score the reference concept with null / zero point in all lines (characteristics).

Therefore, it is possible to compare per-to-per each concept with respect to the reference concept.

In this comparison, it is necessary to answer only one comparison question:

*"The **Characteristic X** of **analyzed Concept** is **Better, equal** or **worse** than **Reference Concept?"***

If the concept is **better**, the concept gains **1 point**. If it is **worse**, it gains **– 1 points.** By the end, if this analyzed concept is **equal** to the reference concept, it gains **0 points** .

It is important to note that this analysis is based on opinions and might be supported by numbers. Nevertheless, this technique is very interesting to evaluate qualitative aspects, such as beauty and robustness sense.

After score all concepts, it is possible to sum up all the points in each column in the bottom line of chart in order to identify the total score of each concept.

Then, the highest scored concepts indicates the most suitable concept in the analysis.

3.2.3   Applying the method

This method is most indicated **for midsize experienced teams (5 to 8 members)** where the members might have either **limited experience in creativity tools been.**

In this case, the **comprehension of the problem is wide**, even though new approaches are needed.

Likewise, this tool is more recommended for **Evaluation and definition** stages of problem solving process.

Problems which required convergence of ideas and concepts in addition to decision making are the most common application of this tools. Therefore, it is possible to converge a wide number of ideas and concepts in a **very small period of time**.

3.2.4   Step-By-Step

Step 1 – Join team members

Step 2 – List problems functions / parameters

Step 3 – List problems solutions, concepts and ideas (identified previously in generation sessions)

Step 4 – Create the Correlation chart (Pugh Diagram Skeleton) where:

- 1st column is problems functions / parameters
- 1st line is problems solutions, concepts and ideas

Step 5 – Choose a reference concept and score zero point to all lines

Step 6 – Analyze the concepts by comparing each function/ parameter of reference concept and the analyzed concept.

It is important to identify whether the analyzed concept is better, equal or worse than the reference concept with respect only to the analyzed function/parameter.

The score scale is:

- +1 – Better
- 0 – Equal
- -1 - Worse

Step 7 – sum up all the points in each column in the bottom line of chart in order to identify the score of each concept.

Step 8 – Sort the concepts by the highest score to the lowest score. The Highest scored concept is the selected concept found in this method.

3.2.5   Examples

This method is unbelievably easy to implement that extremely useful to be applied in any situation that requires selection or decision making.

In this example, I will show you how I used this selection tool in order to decide a new equipment in our workshop. In this case, the decision making tool was used to select a product among available products in the market. Nevertheless, we can easily apply this method for concepts or anything else that you need to choose.

This is an excellent example because it shows comparison between qualitative and quantitative characteristics of products.

Following the method step-by-step, we start defining the criterion and parameters which will be used to compare and select the concepts/products.

In order to analyze the 3 products of our example, we collect basic specifications of each product in addition to define qualitative (uncountable) characteristics.

Based on this comparison chart, it is possible to see that there each product have better characteristics in comparison which each other.

Figure 36

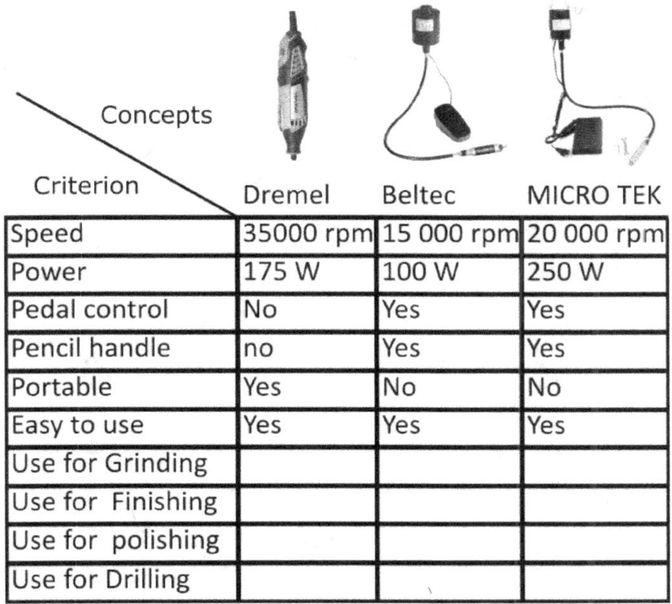

Concepts / Criterion	Dremel	Beltec	MICRO TEK
Speed	35000 rpm	15 000 rpm	20 000 rpm
Power	175 W	100 W	250 W
Pedal control	No	Yes	Yes
Pencil handle	no	Yes	Yes
Portable	Yes	No	No
Easy to use	Yes	Yes	Yes
Use for Grinding			
Use for Finishing			
Use for polishing			
Use for Drilling			

Therefore, we can see that selecting a product among just 3 products is not really a easy task.

Now, when we build the Pugh diagram, thing start changing.

I select the Dremel mandrel as reference; nevertheless, any other reference will lead you to the same result.

After selecting the reference, we score 0 to all of its attributes.

Then, one by one, we compare each criterion of each product with the reference by answering the comparison question.

Figure 37

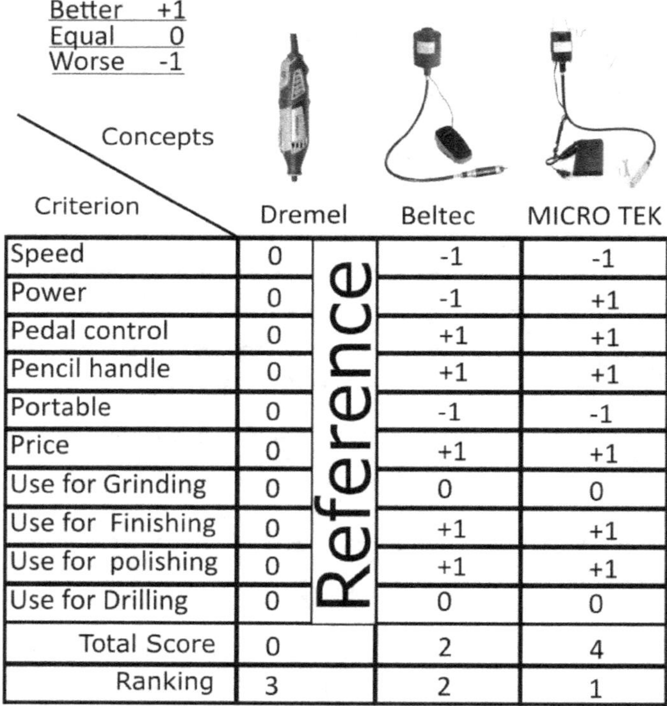

		Dremel	Beltec	MICRO TEK
Better	+1			
Equal	0			
Worse	-1			
Speed		0	-1	-1
Power		0	-1	+1
Pedal control		0	+1	+1
Pencil handle		0	+1	+1
Portable		0	-1	-1
Price		0	+1	+1
Use for Grinding		0	0	0
Use for Finishing		0	+1	+1
Use for polishing		0	+1	+1
Use for Drilling		0	0	0
Total Score		0	2	4
Ranking		3	2	1

For example:

Is the **speed of Beltec better/worse/equal** than the **speed of Dremel** ?

In this case, Beltec speed is worse than Dremel Speed. Therefore, we score **-1** in the cell of beltec – speed.

After score all cells, it is possible to sum up the score of each product and rank the products in accordance with the total score.

In this example, the Micro Tek was selected as the most suitable for our application.

3.2.6   Tricks and recommendations

Ignore to big picture, analyze only the functions

It is common to trying to compare concepts not with respect to the reference. That is mistake that jeopardize de results of the Pugh method.

It is important to note that Pugh Diagram ONLY compares analyzed concept and Reference concepts. Making thing really simple, clean and fast.

Weighted Pugh Diagram

As you might have noticed, the basic Pugh diagram does not take in count how important each criterion is for you.

One way to include this aspect in your analysis is the modified Pugh Diagram which is called Weighted Pugh Diagram.

In this modification, each criterion have a weight of importance.

Everything is exactly the same, apart from the total score. The total score will be calculated by the sum of points multiplied by the weight of importance.

In the same example, I will show you the variation of importance weight in a scale of 1 to 5. Where 5 is a weight of importance which is really important for me.

In this case, I decided that use for Finishing and polishing were the most important criterion (weight 5) in addition to price and speed, which are preferable (weight 3). All the other ordinary criteria were assigned a weight equal to 1.

Figure 38

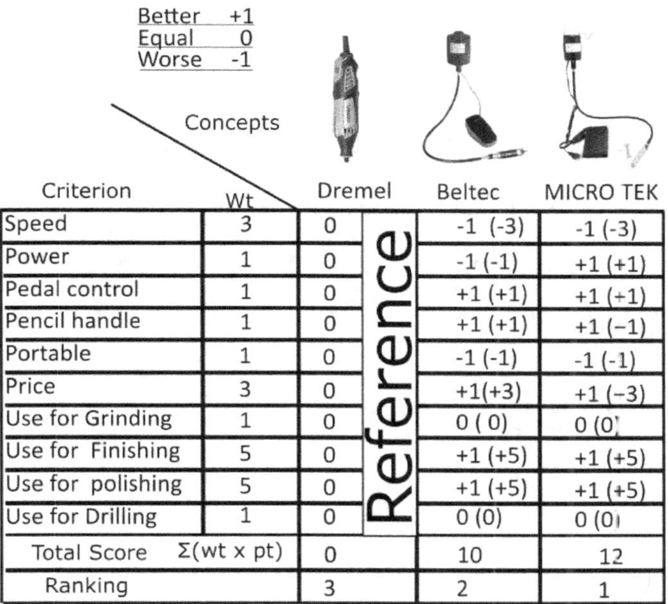

Criterion	Wt	Dremel	Beltec	MICRO TEK
Speed	3	0	-1 (-3)	-1 (-3)
Power	1	0	-1 (-1)	+1 (+1)
Pedal control	1	0	+1 (+1)	+1 (+1)
Pencil handle	1	0	+1 (+1)	+1 (−1)
Portable	1	0	-1 (-1)	-1 (-1)
Price	3	0	+1(+3)	+1 (−3)
Use for Grinding	1	0	0 (0)	0 (0)
Use for Finishing	5	0	+1 (+5)	+1 (+5)
Use for polishing	5	0	+1 (+5)	+1 (+5)
Use for Drilling	1	0	0 (0)	0 (0)
Total Score Σ(wt x pt)		0	10	12
Ranking		3	2	1

Use several selection sessions

In several cases, it is also interesting to make multiple selection sessions in order to create a convergence funnel with high quality result.

It is mainly useful for cases where the amount of quantitative (uncountable) parameters is extremely high.

Therefore, multiple sessions will bring new perspective in each session, making each point of view stronger.

"Creativity requires input, and that's what research is. You're gathering material with which to build."

Gene Luen Yang

The Weighted decision chart is another alternative technique used to select the most suitable concept among available options.

In contrast with Pugh diagram, the Weighted decision chart uses only the quantitative (countable) values in order to score each solution, concept or option to be evaluated.

It is also important to note that no reference concept is needed to be defined in this method, whereas the score is generated in an absolute way.

3.3.1   Definition

The Weighted decision chart is an analytical method that compares the values of each criterion or parameter of concepts in order to score and ranking the most suitable concept.

3.3.2   General overview

This method consists in the generation of a comparison chart where the first line is concepts to be evaluated. In the first column, the main specification, parameters or criterion used to evaluate the options are listed.

Therefore, it is possible to fulfill the column of each option with the respective values of the parameters.

After creating the comparison chart, 3 things need to be done:

- Define importance Weight for each criterion
- Generate the normalized Score for each option
- Sum up the total score of each product

With respect to the importance weight, you can define any scale in accordance with how important the criterion is for you or for your project. I always recommend that you use an scale with 3 steps from 1 to 9. Therefore, it is possible to relevantly highlight the importance in addition to be an easy way to select the importance weight.

For example, you can classify the importance weight as:

- 1 – ordinary importance
- 3– preferable
- 9 – high importance

On the other hand, the normalized score must not depend on the values magnitudes. Otherwise, the criteria would not be comparable.

In this case, it is necessary to use a normalization equation in order to score the values from 0 to 1.

$$Score = \frac{X - V_{min}}{V_{max} - V_{min}}$$

Where:

Vmax is the maximum value among the concepts (in the same row)

Vmin is the minimum value among the concepts (in the same row) which is used as pivot

X is the value of the concept to be scored

For example, the figure below presents the values and score of one criterion.

Figure 39

Criteria	Weight	Concept 1		Concept 2		Concept 3		Max	Min
		Value	Score	Value	Score	Value	Score		
Criterion 1	1	35000	1	15000	0	20000	0,25	35000	15000

It is possible to the concept 1 have the highest value among the evaluated concepts, 35000, while the concept 2 has the lowest value.

As consequence, the normalized score will address 1 to concept 1 and 0 to concept 2.

The intermediate value of concept 3 is scored proportionally to the difference between maximum and minimum values.

After scoring all the concepts and criteria, it is going to be time to sum up the product total score.

In this case, it is necessary to sum the multiplication between the score and weight.

Figure 40

Product specifications/ Selection Criteria	Weight	Concept A		Concept B		Concept C	
		Rating	Weighted rating	Rating	Weighted rating	Rating	Weighted rating
Criterion 1	0.1	2	0.2	4	0.4	4	0.4
Criterion 2	0.2	4	0.8	4	0.8	3	0.6
Criterion 3	0.2	4	0.8	4	0.8	4	0.8
Criterion 4	0.3	3	0.9	3	0.9	5	1.5
Criterion 5	0.2	3	0.6	1	0.2	2	0.4
Total score			3.3		3.1		3.7
Rank		Second		Last		First (optimum)	

(Rating: 5 = excellent, 4 = very good, 3 = good, 2= fair, 1 = poor)

3.3.3 Applying the method

This method is most indicated **for smallsize experienced teams (1 to 3 members)** where the members might have either **limited experience in creativity tools been**.

In this case, the **comprehension of the problem is wide**, even though new approaches are needed.

Likewise, this tool is more recommended for **Evaluation and definition** stages of problem solving process.

Problems which required convergence of ideas and concepts in addition to decision making are the most common application of this tools. Therefore, it is possible to converge a wide number of ideas and concepts in a **very small period of time**.

3.3.4   Step-By-Step

Step 1 – Join team members

Step 2 – List problems functions / parameters

Step 3 – List problems solutions, concepts ard ideas (identified previously in generation sessions)

Step 4 – Create the comparison chart where:

- 1st column is problems functions / parameters
- 1st line is problems solutions, concepts and ideas

Step 5 – Choose importance weight for each criterion

Step 6 – Calculate normalized score for each concept and criterion

Step 7 – sum up all the points in each column in the bottom line of chart in order to identify the score of each concept.

Step 8 – Sort the concepts by the highest score to the lowest score. The Highest scored concept is the selected concept found in this method.

3.3.5 Examples

In order to compare with the Pugh diagram, I will use the same case which I presented to you in the last section.

This example was used to select the most suitable equipment for finishing in our company several years ago.

As well as pugh diagram, we need to collect all the information and specification of products. As a consequence, we start creating a comparison chart.

In contrast with Pugh diagram, all the qualitative (uncountable) specifications, such as beauty and easy to handle, need to be scaled in this phase.

In our example, use for grinding, use for finishing, use for polishing and use for drilling are criteria which reflect the opinion about how easy or how good the product is for an specific application. Therefore, we score each one in a scale from 1 to 5.

Figure 41

Concepts / Criterion	Dremel	Beltec	MICRO TEK
Speed	35000 rpm	15 000 rpm	20 000 rpm
Power	175 W	100 W	250 W
Pedal control	No	Yes	Yes
Pencil handle	no	Yes	Yes
Portable	Yes	No	No
Price	100 usd	50 usd	70usd
Use for Grinding	3	5	5
Use for Finishing	2	5	5
Use for polishing	1	5	5
Use for Drilling	3	1	1

* Scale 1 is difficult and 5 is easy

Another important point in this type of selection tool is the binary criteria, which are defined by positive or negative states. In order to use this method, all positive states are considered 1, while all negative states are considered null or 0.

So, if having a pedal control is a positive criterion, the products which have receive positive value equal to 1, while all the products which haven't, receive negative value equal to 0.

As a result, it was possible to score and rank the evaluated products in addition to rank the most suitable product in accordance with the used criteria and importance weights.

Coincidently, the found ranking was the same as Pugh diagram, where the Microtek was the most suitable for finishing application.

Figure 42

| | | Dremel | | Beltec | | MICRO TEK | | | |
Criteria	Weight	Value	Score	Value	Score	Value	Score	Max	Min
Speed (RPM)	3	35000	1	15000	0	20000	0,25	35000	15000
Power (W)	1	175	0,5	100	0	250	1	250	100
Pedal control (1= yes | 0 = no)	1	0	0	1	1	1	1	1	0
Pencil handle (1= yes | 0 = no)	1	0	0	1	1	1	1	1	0
Portable (1= yes | 0 = no)	1	1	1	0	0	0	0	1	0
Price (USD)	5	100	1	50	0	70	0,4	100	50
Use for Grinding (scale 1 - 5)	1	3	0	5	1	5	1	5	3
Use for Finishing (scale 1 - 5)	5	2	0	5	1	5	1	5	2
Use for polishing (scale 1 - 5)	5	1	0	5	1	5	1	5	1
Use for Drilling (scale 1 - 5)	1	3	1	1	0	1	0	3	1

| Total Score - Σ (weight * score) | | 10,5 | | 13 | | 16,75 | | | |
| Ranking | | 3 | | 2 | | 1 | | | |

* Scale 1 is difficult and 5 is easy

3.3.6 Tricks and recommendations

Convert Yes or no criteria in binary I/O

The weighted decision chart is designed for countable criteria. Therefore, several types of criteria cannot be used in directly.

Yes or no criteria, such as has or does not have some feature, are examples of this exceptions, whereas there is no value to score.

In these cases, it is possible to convert yes or no criteria in binary 1/0 where 1 is assigned to a positive state, such as **have a desired feature** or **do not have an undesired feature**. Likewise, 0 is assigned to the negative state, such as **do not have a desired feature** or **have an undesired feature.**

Transform Qualitative criteria in Quantitative

As commented earlier, qualitative characteristics cannot be directly used in the weighted decision chart.

Nevertheless, it is possible to use a little trick to use qualitative criteria in weighted decision charts.

The qualitative criteria must be transformed in quantitative criteria.

But, how to do so?

All the qualitative criteria need to be scored in accordance with a pre-established scale. For example:

- Percentage of acceptance
- Number of people which in favor of the parameter

- steps score – (1=poor ; 3 – average ; 9=high)

Therefore, if you what to evaluate some concept beautifulness, you can ask for 10 or 100 people whether they like or not. The number of likes divided by the total number (likes/total) is the beautifulness level.

Use Array formulas in Excel or Sheets

Sometimes the calculation of the total score in the weighted decision chart is quite difficult.

For that reason, here I will give you a very good piece of advice:

Use Array Formulas in Excel or Google Sheet.

Ok, but you might have been imagining: HOW?

That is right. The formula will consist in you selecting the sum of whole column of weights multiplied by the whole column of scores. If we have 10 parameter , as exemplified in the chart bellow, the formula will be:

Figure 43

Criteria	Weight	Value	Score
Speed (RPM)	3	35000	1
Power (W)	1	175	0,5
Pedal control (1= yes | 0 = no)	1	0	0
Pencil handle (1= yes | 0 = no)	1	0	0
Portable (1= yes | 0 = no)	1	1	1
Price (USD)	5	100	1
Use for Grinding (scale 1 - 5)	1	3	0
Use for Finishing (scale 1 - 5)	5	2	0
Use for polishing (scale 1 - 5)	5	1	0
Use for Drilling (scale 1 - 5)	1	3	1

=sum(B2:B12*D2:D12)

Instead of press enter, you will have to press ctrl+shift+enter

Then de formula will change to array form.

{=sum(B2:B12*D2:D12)} (in Excel)

Or

=ArrayFormula(sum(B2:B12*D2:D12))

"Creativity comes from a conflict
of ideas"

Donatella Versace

Several projects and conceptions imply on different risk levels. Therefore, another way to evaluate and select a conception consists in the analysis of risk of each concept generated in the creativity process.

3.4.1   Definition

By definition, the risk analysis is a method that measure combined criteria in order to evidence a risk score.

Along the project, the risk score is expected to be reduced, otherwise the high risk indicates that the project need to be declined or shut down.

3.4.2   General overview

In general lines, the risk analysis is a quite simple tool which is possible to be used in several cases.

After generating a concept, it is necessary that you identify threats of your project /conception. In this case, it is recommended that you always identify at least 6 areas, which is called PESTEL:

- **Political**

- Economical
- Social
- Technological
- Environmental
- Legal

Therefore, each identified threat is evaluated by Impact and probability. In other words, it is necessary to identify what is the chances that a threat occurs (probability), in addition to exposing what are the consequences of it (impact).

Risk Value = Impact x Probability

In this case, you can adopt 2 models to analyze:

- Cost based
- Point based

In the cost based risk analysis model, the probability is in percentage while the impact is the amount of money which would be lost if the threat occurs.

For example, imagine that you have a car that cost $ 10000 .00 and you don't have insurance. Then you decide to park in a street in a dangerous neighborhood. The chances of your car is going to be stolen is 20% per each time that you park your car there.

Therefore, the risk value of parking the car with no insurance is $2000 per each time you park your car in such a dangerous neighborhood.

Risk Value = $10000 x 0.2 = $2000.00

On the other hand, this model is quite complicated to be implemented when you are in the very first steps of development.

For that reason, it is possible to use point based risk analysis model. In this model, both the impact and the probability is ranked in a scale from 1 to 5.

In the case of probability, each score indicates how likely the threat can occurs

1- Very unlikely (0 – 1% of changes)
2- Unlikely (1 – 10% of changes)
3- Possible (10 – 50% of changes)
4- Likely (50 – 90% of changes)
5- Very Likely (90 – 100% of changes)

Now with respect to the impact, the score indicates how severe are the consequences of the threat:

1- Negligible
2- Minor
3- Moderate
4- Significant
5- Severe

Therefore, the risk vale vary from 1 to 25 points where it is possible to select ranges of score in which the risk level is acceptable for the project/concept.

It is very common to find risk vs probability vs impact charts which suggest acceptable risk ranges.

Figure 44

Likelihood \ Impact	Negligible	Minor	Moderate	Significant	Severe
Very Likely	Low Med	Medium	Med Hi	High	High
Likely	Low	Low Med	Medium	Med Hi	High
Possible	Low	Low Med	Medium	Med Hi	Med Hi
Unlikely	Low	Low Med	Low Med	Medium	Med Hi
Very Unlikely	Low	Low	Low Med	Medium	Medium

This table can also be represented by range of risk values, where:

- 1 to 6 – Low Risk
- 4 to 12 – Medium Risk-
- 10 to 16 –High Risk-
- >16 – Very high risk

Well, after identifying the risk value of each area of concepts. It is possible to create a chart comparing the total risk, max. risk and risk level of each concept.

Therefore, the concept 1 with the lowest total risk would be the most suitable to be implemented if the threat 5 was treated in order to reduce the risk of concept.

On the other hand, the concept 3 would be the most indicate to be implemented because it has medium risk level and low total risk.

Figure 45

<u>**Probability**</u>

1- Very unlikely (0 – 1% of changes)
2- Unlikely (1 – 10% of changes)
3- Possible (10 – 50% of changes)
4- Likely (50 – 90% of changes)
5- Very Likely (90 – 100% of changes)

<u>**Impact**</u>

1- Negligible
2- Minor
3- Moderate
4- Significant
5- Severe

<u>**Risk Level**</u>

1 to 6 – Low Risk
4 to 12 – Medium Risk
10 to 16 –High Risk-
>16 – Very high risk

Threats	Concept 1			Concept 2			Concept 3		
	Impact	Likelihood	Risk Value	Impact	Likelihood	Risk Value	Impact	Likelihood	Risk Value
Threat 1	1	1	1	1	1	1	1	5	5
Threat 2	1	1	1	1	1	1	1	5	5
Threat 3	5	3	15	5	5	25	3	3	9
Threat 4	3	3	9	3	5	15	3	3	9
Threat 5	1	1	1	1	1	1	1	5	5

Max. Risk	15	25	9
Risk level	High Risk	Very High Risk	Medium Risk
Total Risk	27	43	33

3.4.3 Applying the method

This method is most indicated **for midsize experienced teams (5 to 8 members)** where the members might have either **intermediate experience in creativity tools been**.

In this case, the **comprehension of the problem is wide**, even though new approaches are needed.

Likewise, this tool is more recommended for **Evaluation and definition** stages of problem solving process.

Problems which required convergence of ideas and concepts in addition to decision making are the most common application of this tools. Therefore, it is possible to converge a wide number of ideas and concepts in a **very small period of time**.

3.4.4   Step-By-Step

Step 1 – Join team members

Step 2 – List concepts and problem solutions

Step 3 – list of threats in accordance with PESTEL

Step 4 – Score Impact and probability of each concept threat

Step 5 – Identify the total risk value of each concept

Step 6 – Select the concept with the lowest risk value

"Creativity is the ability to introduce order into the randomness of nature."

Eric Hoffer

4 Development Approaches

As it was discussed before, the innovative methods and creativity methods are strongly linked to prob em solving techniques.

Therefore, section 5.2.5 explains why product development methodologies are so amazing to be used for innovation and creativity approaches.

Ok, but I am neither developing nor innovating products. You might have been asking yourself.

For those who intend to innovate in services, commodities segments or even network and relationships, here goes the greatest news ever.

Everything can be handle as a product in a development process.

In order to better understand which systematic approaches it is possible to find for product development, we classified the types of approaches in 3 groups:

- Product development processes
- Design thinking
- Agile Developments

All those methods have merit and are extremely indicated for different types of situations.

In addition, it is possible to combine those methods and adapt them in accordance with your need.

Here I compiled the most famous methodologies and arranged them in accordance with business maturity level and market maturity level.

Figure 46

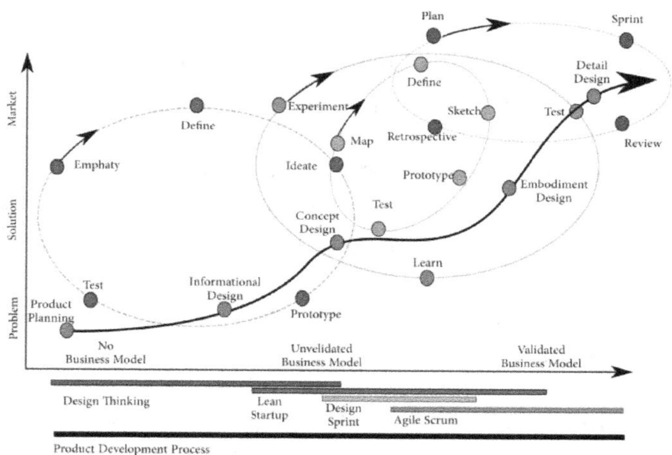

4.1 Product Development Processes

With respect to the product development process, several researchers and companies have been developing and creating their own processes in order to systematize the product development, development finances and processes repeatability.

However, there are several researches which mapped worldwide companies and researches in order to create a generic workflow.

I will highlight the main authors, in my opinion, which created milestones in the field of product development processes:

- Paul and Beitz
- Rozenfeld
- Baxter
- Ullman
- ABNT NBR 13531 for Building projects
- ISO 21500 for general projects

In general, all those authors reached a common sense with respect to the general product development processes.

Although several authors and researchers describe and detail the steps of product development in different ways, we condensed the different syntaxes and simplified in 5 main stages:

1. Product Planning
2. Informational Design
3. Concept Design
4. Embodiment Design

5. Detail Design

In this **product planning stage**, several definitions are established in order to understand:

- Who is the customer
- What is the customer pains
- What is the business models to support the operation
- What is the development strategy
- What are the problem to be solved
- What are the requirements of product
- Who are the development team members

Therefore, it is possible to identify that the delivery of this process stage is:

- Business opportunity
- Customer profile
- business strategy
- project requirement and restrictions
- Estimated Project budget
- Product requirements

It is important to note that the market research is essential to acquire data to support the strategic decision of this stage.

Likewise, the portfolio analysis, needed innovation level, and risk evaluation is also done in this stage.

In order to achieve the main goals of this stage, we recommend a group of analysis tools to help you to clarify the problem, customers pains, customers needs and business:

- Product market matrix
- Analysis of competing companies
- Portfolio matrix
- Need-strength matrix
- Value analysis (value curve from blue ocean strategy)
- Product road map

Figure 47

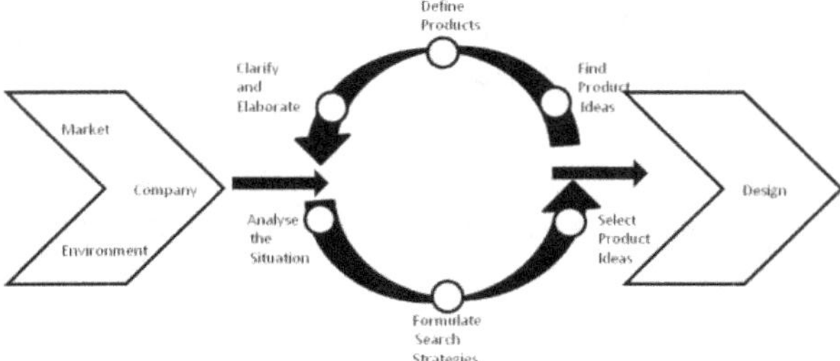

Now in the **Informational Design stage**, the main goal is to organize the data from planning stage and convert it to product specifications, restriction and desired features. In this case, this stage can be described as the translation between customer needs and product specification.

It is very common to see that the informational design is the interface between the marketing and developers, such as designers and engineers. For that reason, this stage is extremely important so that the information does not change along the development flow.

I will give you a very simple example of this stage that expresses the evaluation of simple product, such as mugs.

In this planning stage, it was evidenced that **customers need** a product that:

- have large size
- does not cool the coffee very fast
- does not burn hands

Therefore, the informational stage will translate such qualitative characteristics in product specification. For example:

- **have large size**
    - become
    - **Internal volume between 14 and 18oz**
- **does not cool the coffee very fast becomes**
    - becomes
    - **heat leakage equal lower than 4kJ/h**

- does not burn hands
  - becomes
  - **handle thermal conductivity lower than 0.1 W/(m·K)**

It is clear that the planning and informational design stages are extremely correlated with the initial problem solving stages (understanding and defining).

Moreover, this stage will bring the project planning in consideration, whereas the main tasks, development budget, product cost and industrial costs are deliveries of this stage. It is possible to indicate as deliveries:

- Project Schedule
- Detailed customer segment
- Detailed Project budget
- Detailed Project specification
- Product specification
- Product life-cycle
- Product restrictions
- Development Resources
- Legal Analysis
- Team Definition

In order to achieve the main goals of this stage, we recommend a group of analysis tools to help you to clarify the project, translate needs in specification, detail project tasks, budget and cost:

- QFD (Quality Function Deployment)
- Make or Buy Analysis
- Gantt chart
- WBS (Working Breakdown Structure)
- Pert diagram
- Creativity Methods
- Resource Allocation analysis
- Value stream analysis
- Economical Feasibility Analysis
- Creativity tools
- Concept selection and decision making tools

In contrast, it can be also identified that in the **Concept Design stage** is expected to generate ideas and select the concept for the product or solution. This stage is also called ideation stage consists in:

- Update project plan
- Generate and selects a functional product concept
- Generate and select a Aesthetical and ergonomic product concepts
- Create feature for the product specifications
- Define Suppliers and partners for the project
- Estimate manufacturing processes in a macro scale
- Update feasibility analysis
- Fabricate functional prototypes and mockups
- Evaluate customer perception

This stage is one of the most important stages in the product development, whereas it generates ideas to solve the customer problem in addition to establish the concept to be implemented.

As delivery, this stage aim to:

- Define working principle
- Define concepts
- Define simplified product Design
- Define general Bill of Material (BOM
- Define Supplier list
- Define product Layout

Therefore, all creativity are highly recommended to be used in this stage in addition to concept selection and decision making methods. Likewise, we also recommend you to use:

- FMEA (Failure Mode and Effect Analysis)
- Make-or-buy analysis
- Cost analysis
- Economical feasibility analysis
- Design of Experiments
- FTA (Fault Tree Analysis)
- 3D printing and Prototyping

After the definition of concepts and preliminary evaluation in the market, **Embodiment design Stage** starts. In this stage, the preliminary calculations, simulations, optimization studies are done.

It is noteworthy that the embodiment design stage is no found in all literatures, being often included in the detailed design stage.

Nevertheless, the main goal of this stage is to improve the concept and reduce weak spots.

For example, as the concept does not need to have the material, manufacturing processes defined in the concept design stage, the embodiment design stage will address such matters, generating studies that will select the suitable manufacturing process, material and general dimensions.

As delivery, this stage aim to:

- Product Structure
- 3D model
- Definition of manufacturing processes
- Selection of material family
- Planning and selection of manufacturing resources
- Development of suppliers
- Detailed Costs
    - Overhead
    - Direct material
    - Logistics

- o   Indirect material
- o   Manufacturing
- o   Tooling
- o   Machine
- o   Infrastructure

Therefore, all the major project details will gain body in order to be implemented. Likewise, we also recommend you to use:

- FMEA (Failure Mode and Effect Analysis)
- Detailed Product Structure
- Simulation tools
- Make-or-buy analysis
- Cost analysis
- Economical feasibility analysis
- Design of Experiments
- FTA (Fault Tree Analysis)
- 3D printing and Prototyping

The last stage of this generic process is the **Detailed design Stage**. It consists in the stage where the final touches of design are performed. After this stage, the product/service is launched so that this stage is vital for the product.

In general lines, it is possible to indicate general tasks for this stage where the main goal is to prepare the concept to be produced/launched. Therefore, it is possible to establish as the main deliveries:

- Component drawings/specification
- Tolerance analysis
- Tooling design
- Try-out and product testing
- Product strength and safety testing
- Maintenance planning
- Technical support planning
- Manufacturing machine specification
- Manufacturing planning
- CAPEX
- Inspection sheets
- Economical feasibility analysis
- Product homologation /certification
- Definition of Suppliers and commodities
- Package design
- Product reliability testing
- Quality assurance
- Adjust product to legislation and standards

After this stage, the product/ service is launched and the post-sales and manufacturing become responsible to maintain the product in accordance with the specification design.

4.1.1   Tips and Tricks

Put energy and money in the initial stages of development

It is noteworthy that project and product development processes have long duration in several moments. In addition, there are plenty of costs involved in the project in order to accomplish it, such as tooling cost, labor hours, et cetera.

For that reason, several researches and professional in the field identified the distribution of costs during the project.

Amazingly, it is possible to see that the preliminary stages of product development process cause the highest impact on the total development if an eventual error occurs.

It means that small error in the planning and design might jeopardize the entire operation, while small errors in production and supply chain can be tolerated and absorbed by the operation.

Figure 48

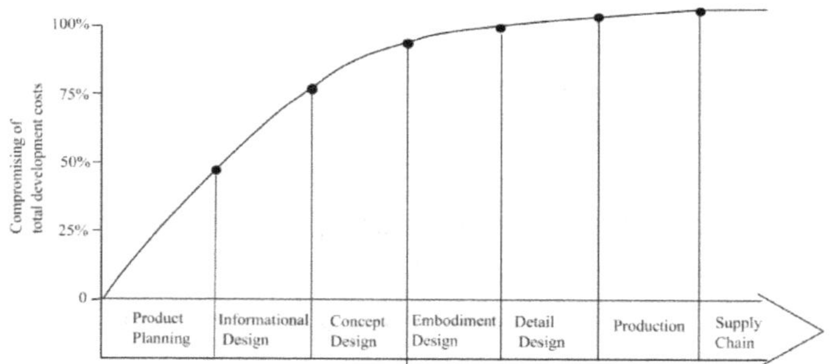

Don't Lose focus

As commented before, product development is usually a marathon, not a sprint. For that reason, it is extremely important to rely on the planning and informational design.

Project changes during the development, of course. Nevertheless, the guidelines defined in the planning and informational design are the compass of the design.

It is important to note that this method is the most used by successful companies and rely on the method will bring suitable results.

If you want flexibility, thus. Create checkpoints in the project that allows you to change the scope, main characteristics of project or even kill the project.

I recommend you to create 2 checkpoints by process stage. Therefore, it is going to be possible to adjust the direction of stage in order to update technology, legislation, Customer profile, among other characteristics.

Use a project management tool

In order to manage the project in addition to follow tasks, project management tools are remarkably useful.

In this subject, there are really thousand apps and software that might help you to do so. Nonetheless, I will bring you the most interesting and famous in the area.

- MS Project
- Minerva
- GanttProject
- TeamGantt for online application
- Google Tables

Those tools are excellent because they are capable of:

- Create Gantt Diagrams
- Create Task Schedule
- Create PERT (Program Evaluation and Review Technique) analysis in order to estimate possible, optimistic and pessimistic estimations for due date
- Create CPM(Critical Path Method) Analysis

- Create labor load analysis
- Estimate project costs
- Controls project resources and project progression

In contrast with the product development process, the design thinking is an design methods that is based on iterations and become very popular from 2010 on. As example of companies that explicitly adopt design thinking to solve problems and generate value, we can list IBM, Itaú, Bradesco, Robert Bosch, Whirlpool, Mapfre, TOTVS, Linx, among other.

The general idea in the design thinking is to constantly capture the pain of customers besides generating and testing fast solutions.

In spite of several flavors of design thinking process, most of them are based in a double diamond creativity method, presented in the previous chapter, and can be described in 5 stages:

- Empathy
- Define
- Ideate
- Prototype
- Test

Those 5 stages are high influenced by "Herbert Simon, The Sciences of the Artificial (3rd Edition), 1996".

Figure 49

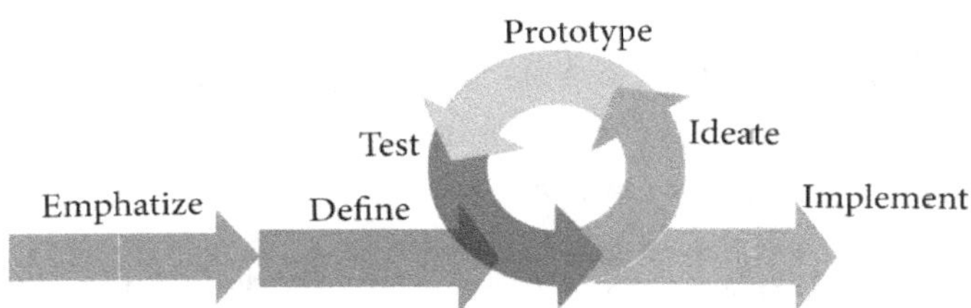

It is possible to identify that this development model is highly indicated to understand and develop solutions for problems, even though there are no business model established yet.

In the **Empathy stage**, the main goal is to capture the pain of customer and identify opportunities that can be solved by the design thinking method. It is also possible to say that Empathy stage is all about find ways to make the life of your customer easier.

It is possible to establish the correlation with the empathy stage with the understanding stage of problem solving method, which was explained in the previous chapter.

As result this stage delivers the essence of problem, problems, or problem systems which are needed to be addressed by the design thinking team.

Now the **Define stage**, the main goal is to define the problems and sub-problems, understanding approaches and collect data to support understanding of problem and customer.

In this stage, it is possible to use systematic and non-systematic approaches, even though I always recommend systematic approaches.

In this case, the most interesting methods that I would suggest are:

- Functional Analysis
- Parametric Analysis
- Product-market Matrix
- Heuristic Redefinition

It is also interesting to use Quality Tools (presented in the next chapter) in order to better understand the whole picture, such as:

- QFD (Quality Function Deployment)
- Dimensions of Quality
- 7 Quality Tools

Therefore, the main delivery of this stage is the specification of problems, needs of customers and restrictions which the project will have to address.

In the other hand, the **Ideate stage** is the moment where the ideas are elaborated in order to create solutions and alternatives to solve the problem which was identified before.

This method is also correspondent to the concept design of product development process, whereas it is where ideas are sketched and designed. It is important to note that this part considers any type of design, such as aesthetic, graphical and functional.

It is normally composed by 2 sub-stages: Divergent ideation and convergent ideation. Where the divergent step is driven by "thinking outside the box" philosophy, while the convergent ideation is driven by the "idea funnel" philosophy.

In the first case any method of systematic creativity tool is worthwhile, while the second case is recommended to use concept selection tools, instead.

On the other hand, **Prototype stage** consists in the materialization of the idea, where it is possible to establish different levels of prototype in accordance with each development iteration.

In general way, It is possible to divide the prototype stage in:

1. Aesthetic mockups
2. Functional Mockups
3. Aesthetic prototypes
4. Functional Prototypes

5. Minimal Lovable Product
6. Minimal Valuable Product
7. Launching product

After prototype stage, the **Test stage** will put the prototypes in check in order to proof functionality, aesthetic acceptance, customer experience, manufacturing viability, and other feasibilities of operation.

This process repeats in several iterations until the customer pains are suitably solved and the product is launched.

Although the product launching, several companies continue using design thinking in order to update the product and solving bugs.

4.2.1 Tips and Tricks

Use a tracking system

It is usual that people whom is engaged with design thinking try not to be attached to rules, schedules or systematic.

That is a complete mistake, because the design thinking is in matter of fact a systematic approach to solve problems and develop new concepts, opportunities and solutions.

Therefore, before you engage yourself in design thinking projects, establish a tracking system method.

It can be actually anything, varying from notebooks, kanban boards, checklists apps, Kankan apps like trello, spreadsheets like excel or google sheets, among others.

I can ensure you that the best system to chose is the one which you actually use.

So, I will put a list some tools that I strongly recommend you to check:

- Spreadsheets – Example of Falconni Method for Spreadsheet Tracking
    - https://drive.google.com/file/d/1-TRoKvkevdYrMcERZ8rIQ6wIUQ02d4EI/view?usp=sharing
- Trello
- Google Table
- GanttProject
- Kanban boards and post its for design thinking

Your Habits will Empower you

Develop new things are difficult. In addition, change the routine is even harder.

Why? Simple, people tend to stay in the comfort zone because is more convenient for them.

In order to incorporate new task into your daily basis, check the rule of 10 seconds.

It means that, you have to create obstacles to make difficult to start a task (non productive or that you want to remove). This task should take more than 10 seconds you to start. My experience says that a task that you really don't want need to take more than 1 minute to start so that you will dropped it in a light speed.

On the other hand, things that you want to incorporate to your daily routine need to be facilitated. Thus, you have to be able to start doing the task in less than 10 seconds.

Here we are!

Start to incorporate Design thinking tasks in your daily basis in a small amount, such as 30 minutes/day. Each week, increase half hour until you start working and fully engaged in the design thinking for all your projects.

On the other hand, several other design approaches have been developed along the yeas in order to accelerate the product launching and increase productivity.

I separated the 3 most famous tools which are considered Agile methodology :

- Sprint
    - Famous for being used by Google projects
    - The most interesting literature of this method is

Knapp, J., Zeratsky, J. and Kowitz, B., 2016. **Sprint: How to solve big problems and test new ideas in just five days**. Simon and Schuster.

- Scrum
    - Famous for being used in Programming and software based companies
    - The most interesting literature of this method is

Sutherland, J. and Sutherland, J.J., 2014. **Scrum: the art of doing twice the work in half the time**. Currency.

- Lean Startup
    - Famous for being applied in several companies in Silicon Valley

- o The most interesting literature of this method is

Ries, E., 2011. **The lean startup: How today's entrepreneurs use continuous innovation to create radically successful businesses**. Currency.

It is important to note that all those methodologies have their own characteristics and several studies and companies also modify and mix them in order to obtain different results.

For that reason, it is good that you learn more about all of these methods in order to extract all the protein that is aligned with your goals.

As the main goal of this book is to introduce you those techniques, I will show you a summary of each one of those. However, I strongly recommend you to read the suggested literature in order to generate a deeper knowledge of the subject.

4.3.1   Sprint

The Sprint design is an very interesting technique which has a lead time equal to 5 days. Nevertheless, some companies might indicate longer lead time for each sprint because of their internal needs.

It is noteworthy that this method is a branch of design thinking and consist in a 5 stage cycle:

- Map
- Sketch
- Decide
- Prototype
- Test

Figure 50

In the **Mapping stage**, you can find the kickoff of the project, where the team identifies the project goals in short and long term in addition to the relative deliveries that it is expected to achieve.

It is possible to establish a parallel approach for this phase where data is collected, problem is defined and subsystems are also created.

Now the **Sketch stage**, the ideas are generated by either non-systematic tools or systematic tools, as presented previously.

The main goal in this stage is to generate ideas, therefore all creativity tools can be widely used.

Nowadays, several designers also create 3D models of concepts in order to better explain and represent their ideas. Nonetheless, it might be tendentious because of difference between quality of each 3D model.

For that reason, I strongly recommend that all ideas stay in low profile and abstract until the beginning of prototype and test.

In the other hand, the **Decide stage** is all about funnel the large amount of ideas generated in the previous stage.

In this moment, Concept Selection and decision making tools are terrific to help the project team to decide which concept or concepts will be prototyped and tested.

After selecting the concepts which goes to the next phases. A storyboard is created in order to explode tasks and detail how the concept will be fabricated.

The **Prototype stage** consists in the materialize the concept in a way that the concept can be evaluated.

This moment is normally branded by the slogan "Fake It Till' You Make It". This is because the first iterations of sprint will imply on mockups, mock experiences and functional prototypes (which usually looks like "Franksteins"). And the general idea is to validate the features of the concept based on the opinion of internal customers, external customers and even design team.

This stage also includes preparation for the test stage, such as test schedule, quality checklist, process assembly sheets , etc.

After prototype stage, the **Test stage** will submit the prototype to different conditions, passing by restricted customer group, pilot production, extended customer groups, for example.

It is important that the test results in leaning and the decisions need to be addressed in the map stage, when either a new iteration will start with new goals or the project will be killed.

As this process is iterative, each iteration will increase the mature level of product and eventually generate a MVP (Minimal Valuable Product) and final Product.

Usually, it is possible to address test valuations based iteration:

1. Aesthetic mockups
2. Functional Mockups
3. Aesthetic prototypes
4. Functional Prototypes
5. Minimal Lovable Product
6. Minimal Valuable Product
7. Pilot production
8. Launching product

4.3.2   Scrum

The Scrum is an method that was mostly influenced by Jeff Sutherland and widely applied in Software development, small companies and startup companies. It is noteworthy that this method is a hybrid branch of design thinking that mix Design Thinking and Sprint in an organized framework. In simple lines, the iterative cycle of scrum consist in 4 steps:

- **Plan**
- **Sprint**
- **Review**
- **Retrospective**

Figure 51

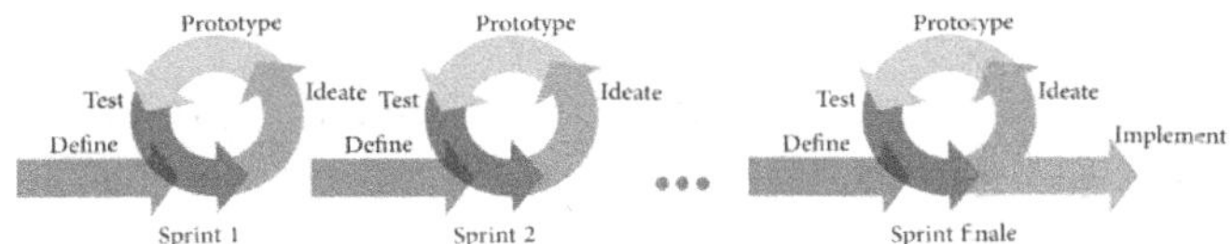

In other Scrum flavors, the first step to implement scrum is to **define the main project roles**. Then the feedback loop starts (iteration cycle) where the common stages are:

- Create Product Backlog
- Sprint Planning meeting
- Sprint Cycle
- Sprint Review / Demo
- Sprint Retrospective

The **Main Scrum Roles** are:

Product Owner (PO): Who decides WHAT to do and WHY.

The main responsibility of Product Owner is to be the Guardian of Product Vision and the Project Deliveries. This role also consists in the management of the Product Backlog or Product Requirements in addition with the interaction with Customers.

In big projects, it is possible to have several POs in order to achieve subsystems or SubProducts.

Scrum Master: Who is focused in HOW to work better.

This role aim to organize and manage the project in order to optimize results in daily basis. The Scrum master coach the team in addition to interact with stakeholders in order to remove obstacles, solving conflicts and managing resources .

Team or Squaq: Who actually DO the development and work.

The team is composed by team members who have complementary skills to develop and deliver the project or product.

In this case, who decide how to achieve the goals and product increment are the team members with help of Scrum Master.

In this moment, the customer pain are converted in knowledge so that the problem can be transformed in tasks to be addressed in the experiment stage.

In general lines, the team size is recommended to be between 3 and 9 people. Otherwise, the organization become more bureaucratic and the team lose focus of PO product vision.

The **Product Backlog stage** consists in the moment where the customer needs materialize in product Requirements, Defects and features of product. In this backlog, it is described what it is expected to be achieved as product vision.

As a consequence, these requirements are converted in subsystems or features in order to generate Sprints or short project .

It is important to note that the meaning of Sprint in this context is different from the Sprint method which I exposed to you before. In this context, the sprint consists in the group of tasks that are needed to achieve a requirement from backlog in a short period of time (usually 1 to 2 weeks).

After defining the Product backlog, the team and product owner agreed on the sprint goal during the **Sprint Planning**. Therefore, the tasks, task goals and their priorities are defined and incorporated to a **Sprint Backlog**. It is important to note that the Sprint Backlog indicates when the task is considered done and what are the expected deliveries of each task.

In the **Sprint Planning stage**, the most important topics to be addressed are:

- **Why is this Sprint Valuable?**

While Product Owner indicate how the sprint increased value of product, the Scrum Team defines the **Sprint Goal** and how the sprint is valuable to Stakeholders.

- **What are the Sprint Goals ?**

In this moment, the required resources and estimated deadlines become the focus of discussion in order to make the sprint goal achievable.

- **What can be Done in this sprint?**

In this topic, the Product Owner and developers select an item from Product backlog to be addressed in the current sprint.

- **How will the chosen work get Done?**

After the definition of Sprint goal, the item of the product backlog is decomposed in small tasks in addition to distributed among Scrum Team in accordance with each one expertise, experience and availability.

By the end, it is possible to distribute tasks and responsibility in order to follow the sprint progress and identify the blockages or struggling of team members during the execution of each task.

Therefore, the **Sprint Cycle** flows in a way that the team need only to complete the assigned tasks.

Normally, the follow-up of these tasks occurs in a Scrum Board, which are also called Kanban Boards.

Figure 52

Sprint Backlog	Design		Development		Testing		Done
	Doing	Ready	Doing	Ready	Doing	Ready	

The sprint cycle have no rigid molds, as the team experts and scrum master are free to define HOW is the best way to **do**, **test** and **release** the features and tasks.

Nevertheless, it's a common sense that the sprint cycle follows a Design Thinking Architecture, such as:

- Empathy
- Define
- Ideate
- Prototype
- Test

Another approach that several teams around the world adopts is to define **Daily sprints**, where the scrum master assumes a role of the Sprint owner and split the sprint goal in several small goals that can be achieved each 1 to 2 days.

During the sprint, it is important that **Sprint Goal DOES NOT CHANGE**. Otherwise the whole method collapse and the project enters in a stagnation spiral.

The end of the Sprint period is marked by the **Sprint Review**, where the tasks, goals, deliveries, blockages and project conflicts that occurs during the sprint are reviewed.

In the **Sprint Review**, the performance of the team and progress of project toward the Product Goal are discussed.

It is important that the Sprint review is not limited to presentation, whereas action plan need to be implemented in order to avoid project issues to occur again.

In order to continue improving the development, the **Sprint Retrospective** indicates the learning lessons and go deep in a discussion about how each individual, process, tool, definition or even external noises affects efficiency of sprint.

Note that if the Sprint does not deliver what is expected, a new sprint is created to adjust and develop the tasks to achieve the sprint goal.

4.3.3   Lean Startup

The Lean Startup is an method that was mostly influenced by Eric Ries and directed to small companies and startup companies. It is noteworthy that this method is a branch of design thinking and consist in only 3 stage cycle:

- Experiment or Building
- Test or measure
- Learn

Figure 53

The **Learn stage** consists in the stage where the opportunities are identified in addition to recording development status in order to adjust the project scope for the next iteration.

In this moment, the customer pain are converted in knowledge so that the problem can be transformed in tasks to be addressed in the experiment stage.

In the **Experiment stage**, the main goal is to generate ideas, design and materialize conceptions which were previously identified in the Learning stage.

For software and apps, this method is extremely useful because of speed of obtaining something tangible and sellable .

Now the **Test stage**, is the moment where all the data is collected in addition to evaluate concepts and designs.

It is good to highlight that this stage also consists in collect and analyze market data in order to generate results which will be interpreted and processed in the learning stage. Therefore, opportunities can be identified and concepts can be adjusted, modified or even killed.

This process repeats in several iterations until the customer pains is suitably solved.

4.3.4   Tips and Tricks Lacking figures

Use BurnDown and BurnUp Chart

In order to follow-up the progress of the sprint, it is possible to use BurnDown and BurnUp Charts.

The Burndown chart consists in the chart that illustrate the amount of tasks in the sprint as a function of the time. In this method, the easiest way to identify a normal strategy is to create a straight line or projected line from the quantity of Sprint tasks in the day 0 and the last day of Sprint. Therefore, the end of diagram is expected to be 0 tasks in the last sprint day.

It is expected that the tasks follows the normal line in order to optimize the sprint. This chart is an amazing tool in order to optimize resources and improve predictability and estimation skill of Team and the Scrum Master.

Figure 54

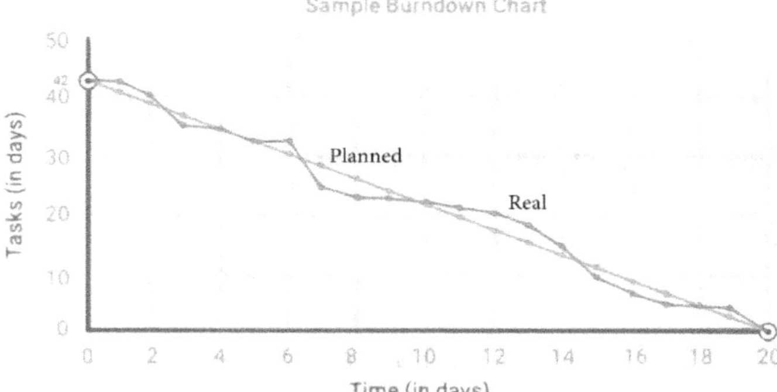

On the other hand, the BurnUp chart represent the progress of completed tasks in an opposite way. There is no tasks at the day 0 of sprint and the projected line goes up along the days.

Figure 55

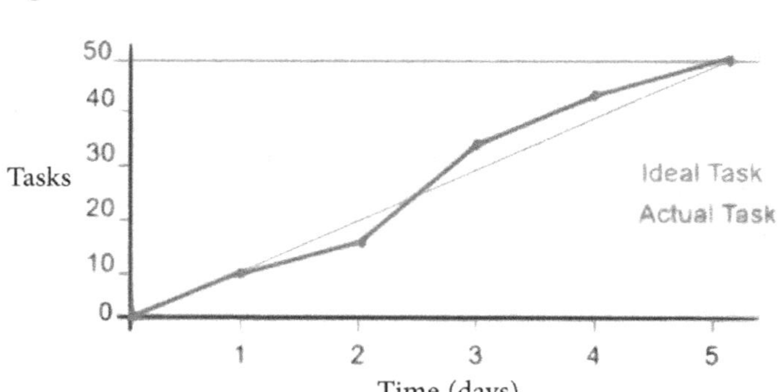

Additionally, the amount of work or tasks during the sprint can vary, creating a new projection line.

In both of cases, it is possible to follow-up the progress of sprint in addition to identify struggling points where the scrum master need to act to help the project to flow.

It is also interesting to note that another goal of both methods is to identify if the sprint progress is adherent to the planning.

There is no pot of gold at the end of rainbow

Each method is slightly different and helps you in a different way.

Unfortunately, applying the methods is the only way to decide which method is the most suitable for you. In addition, it will also depends on the project, leadtime, maturity stage, innovation level, experience of team and business model.

Moreover, it is possible to indicate sprints for shallow incremental innovations (SII) and Kaizens, while lean startups and design thinking for deep incremental innovation (DII). It is also possible to use product development processes and design thinking for continuous disruptive innovation (CDI).

"The most creative act you will ever undertake is the act of creating yourself."

Deepak Chopra

5 QUALITY TOOLS - The most precious asset of yours is your client

It is interesting to note that both customer driven services and quality driven services put the customer as an important piece of a complex beautiful machine.

Collecting data from customers are excellent tool to guide your next steps in the perceived quality and decide how to prioritize your investments.

5.1 Uncontrolled Clients

This type of client is very interesting and as any other client, they invest into your company. They believe in your work and sometimes have periodic orders.

The problem in this type of client is the fact that they don't share information and they don't want you to understand their needs and help them to bu ld products.

They have the relationship control over you. In addition, they can even move to other competitor without hesitation.

In other words, the risk that you will face in front of this client is high. So, I recommend that you keep this clients running on while you develop new relationship with another client that you have control.

5.2   Controlled Clients

Since the first industrial revolutions, one thing is certain. Collaborative work and collaborative design had been ensuring manufactures to grow as satellite of their clients.

For example, an automotive industries are nothing without engine factories or wheels factories.

Therefore, it is possible to say that a controlled client is the one who **shares project and design responsibility**.

You understood what I am going to arrive, didn't you?

In the moment that you start helping you clients, you become their partner. Therefore, Quality driven services start to become reality.

In order to achieve challenging targets, powerful tools are required. I will present to you the 3 tools that will allow you to understand your controlled client.

- 8 Dimensions
- QFD – Quality Function Deployment
- Blind Experience

In general way, the perceived quality has 8 dimensions,

- Dimension 1: Performance
- Dimension 2: Features
- Dimension 3: Reliability
- Dimension 4: Conformance
- Dimension 5: Durability
- Dimension 6: Serviceability
- Dimension 7: Aesthetic
- Dimension 8: Perception

As we learned, each customer sees the worlds from one different window, but all of them instinctively take attention to all dimensions, even though this dimension is not important to them.

Performance indicates that the product works in the way it was supposed to work. It is important to note that this is not an obvious matter. You have to considers that in spite of errors of your customer design, success of your service will depend on how well the product works or how well prototyped parts assembly each other.

In this case, try-out tests make all the sense before a final deliver.

Features are things that generates value to the product. This dimension is the one you should exploit the most.

Each design has special characteristics to become unique. Each designer has his/her either.

As features are small parts of design, you can improve it progressively and incrementally, such as we presented in the strategy of Customer driven services.

Reliability is the things and elements which make your customer to trust and rely on your services. This is a branding characteristics that is fundamentally defined during the first services or by indication.

In this case, deliver features that ensure that your product is reliable make plenty of difference.

I will give you one example. Once, I implement the policy of delivering a dimensional/assembly/tensile testing report in the delivery product/parts. In this case, the customer which I aimed to increase reliability has the dimensional/mechanics characteristics as his top priorities. Instantaneously after implement this policy, they changed the behavior and start openly discuss design and projects with our team.

Gain the trust of whom you want to be partner.

Conformance is the characteristic that technical and expert customers like the most. It is related to the precision and how alike the physical object is from the design and 3D model, for example.

In this case, it is important to ensure a suitable conformance. But pursuit of great conformance usually implies on equipment, training and labor investment.

In this matter, you have to realize that most of **ordinary customers don't care about conformance, but performance**.

In addition, controlled clients share responsibility with you, giving you opportunity to adjust the design in order to absorb tolerances and fabrication errors.

Durability is a factor that is highly enhanced to cost and price. This dimension describes how long or how much the product will take.

In this case, nothing is eternal, but disposable thing sounds cheap in customer mind.

Therefore, you will have to find the balance between disposable and eternal levels.

What I recommend in here is to start with disposable materials, configurations and poor finishes in the internal try-outs. And use a good materials and practices in the external (showing to client).

Never let your client keep a poor try-out (prototype) even it is at the beginning of your development.

Further information can be found in material strength books (very technical) or in the book Make it stunning.

Aesthetic is the dimension that make the eyes of everyone shine. In this dimension, the first thing that you have been imagine is a polish surface.

Of course, some one that is also familiar with 3D printing techniques will also say. Use acetone or methyl Ethyl Ketone (MEK) in an ABS object.

By 15 years of experience in 3D printing segment and being a winner of the international award of best 3D printing research, I am affray to say that it is a rookie mistake.

I will explain it to you so that you will understand. I am not against solvent vapor attack (such as acetone vapor). I am saying that most of customers don't like it.

They are looking for innovation and combination of senses. And because there are infinite types of finishing, materials, textures, techniques and tacti e elements, the both your mind and your customer mind can freely flight and create an unique texture feature that will make your customer product special.

Serviceability is the dimension which indicates how easy the product is to be fixed or repaired.

It is interesting to note that in spite of the importance o this dimension. I can say by experience that most of customers don't care about this quality dimension in the stages of the product development.

Nevertheless, a suitable design of multiple parts product, in addition to joints, fasteners, snap fits make the difference between amateur and professional designs.

Quite many recommendations about this matter can be learned in books of machine design. It will help you to have ideas about attachment systems in the book "Make It Stunning".

Perception this dimension is the most important dimension in most of cases. This dimension can also be called Wow dimension.

Now is the moment that you use all the powerful knowledge about your customer and put into the product. Fabricating personalized things for your customers make them feel important and special.

Additionally, this dimension is widely cover by the co-responsibility approach, where you help your client to design the product.

That is one of the reasons why a solid relationship with you customer is so important.

> "If your customers like you (your services), thing that you make will easily please them.
>
> If your customer do not like you(your services), any work that you make will not please them."

Ok, now that you learned what are the 8 dimensions of quality, how does each dimension can be used in your favor?

One of the most common methods to put in practice is 8 dimensions map. In this map, it is possible to evaluate the effect of feature on your customers.

This method is a powerful tool to identify how good is the impact of a developed feature on your customer, and you can do it in 3 steps.

Therefore, you evaluate how much your customer value each one of 8 dimensions in a scale from 1 to 5.

Analyze value the feature or product in accordance with each one of 8 dimensions in a scale from 1 to 5

Find the impact coefficient by multiplying the values of features and customers.

Values higher than 9 indicate that the feature will cause good impression on your customers in that dimension. Values lower than 9 will probably be ignored.

For example, once I implemented a new rubbery texturized finishing as part of the brand new development of a customer design. I evaluated a ordinary customers who aimed to proof a design concept.

In this case, the strongest characteristics of the feature that I was implementing were aesthetic and feature

After mapping both the customer and the feature, I was able to predict that the customer perception about the product would be Aesthetic Feature and Perception.

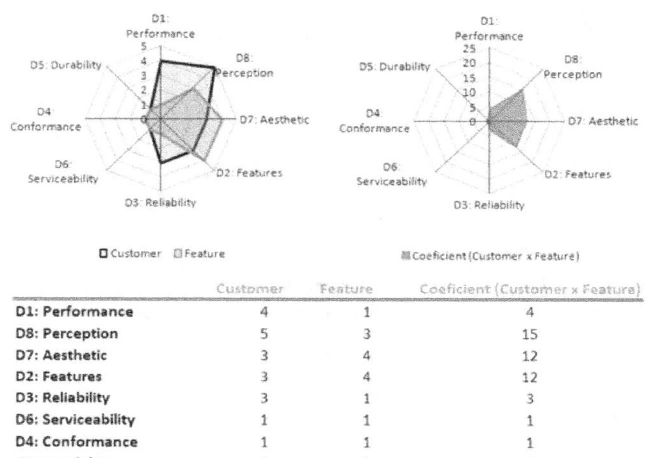

	Customer	Feature	Coeficient (Customer x Feature)
D1: Performance	4	1	4
D8: Perception	5	3	15
D7: Aesthetic	3	4	12
D2: Features	3	4	12
D3: Reliability	3	1	3
D6: Serviceability	1	1	1
D4: Conformance	1	1	1
D5: Durability	1	1	1

Thus, what does it mean?

Delivering an creative design or product in terms of aesthetic and tactility which make his product different from his past experiences would achieve 12 times more impact than fabricates a perfect object in terms of dimensions and strength.

Well, you can easily see that 8 dimensions might imply on quite many qualitative characteristics ,

characteristics with cannot be counted or measured in numbers.

For example, you evaluate a customer that indicates that he want that his product/object is beautifully shinny. Certainly you identified that he considers aesthetic and feature as the most important dimensions of quality.

But, how shinny must your object be, for example?

If you make it right once, how can you repeat the result? How can you measure when you can stop?

In order to quantify these uncountable (qualitative) characteristics, I will show you the tool that revolutionized automotive industry: Quality Function Deployment (QFD).

5.4   Quality Function Deployment (QFD)

This tool is one of the most useful approaches to connect marketing analyses and technical specification. It correlates the needs and expectations of customers and the technical characteristics of design.

In other words, this method indicates that, **beautifully shinny** can be **measured by roughness and reflectance**, while it can be **achieved by Surface treatments** (such as chemical attack, thermal attack, coating, glazing, among others).

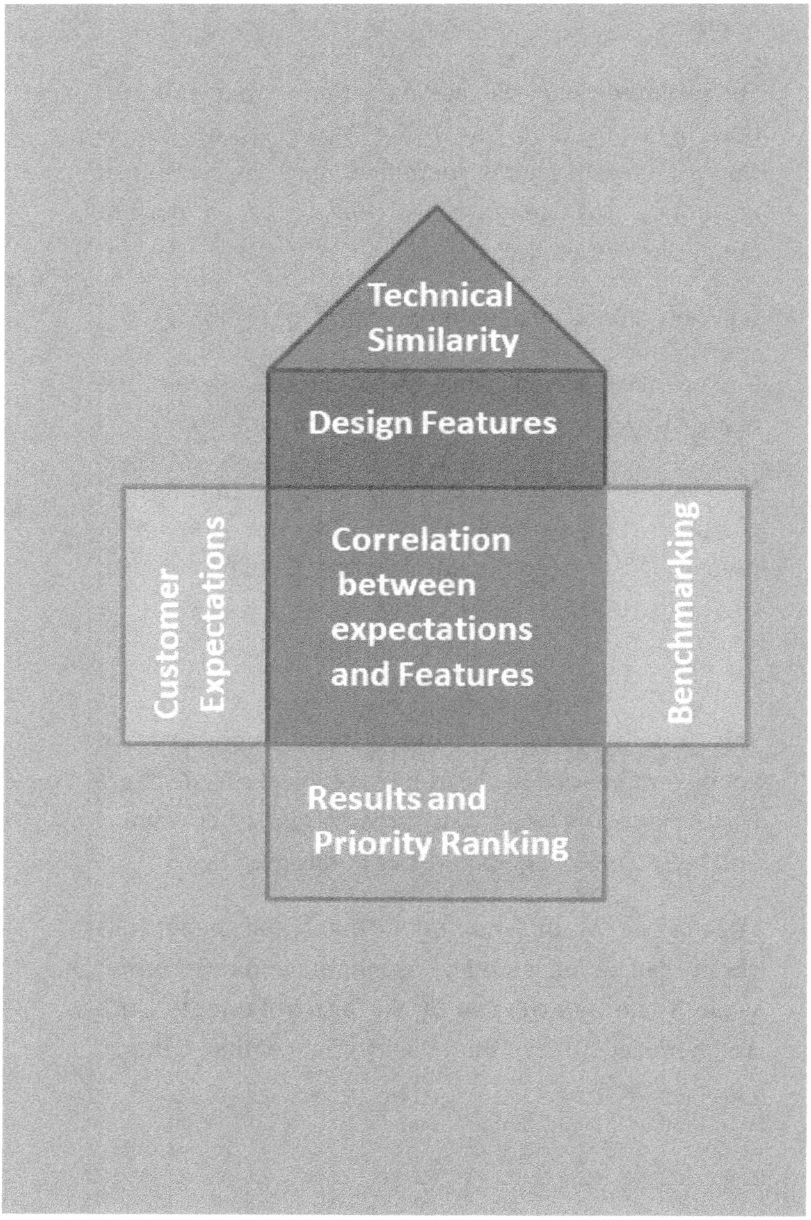

Technical Similarity
Design Features
Customer Expectations
Correlation between expectations and Features
Benchmarking
Results and Priority Ranking

In a simple way, the QFD can be described in 3 main parts:

- Customer expectations
- Design features
- Correlation between expectations and Features

Illustrating the application of this table, I will show you the analysis of a simple Mug which a client of mine asked for my help to develop.

I this case, the customer expected that Mug should be:

- big
- Fit in the car support
- Look like himself
- Don't drop coffee into car because of motion
- Warm hand
- Don't burn hands
- Keep coffee warm

In contrast, what did I have into my toolbox to develop this product?

I could define:

- Internal mug volume (Oz or ml)
- Size (cubic feet or mm^3)
- Color

- Material
- Shape
- Coating and painting
- Insulation
- Lid

Perfect, knowing the importance that each expectation of my client, I could correlate the design feature and customer expectations .

I found that the 3 most important thing in the design from the technical point of view were:

- Shape
- Type of material
- Insulation

In contrast, this exactly design characteristics made my customer to see that the mug:

- Don't burn hands
- Keep coffee warm
- Look like myself

Figure 58

Strong Relationship - 9
Medium Relationship - 3
Weak Relationship -1
no relationship -

			Business Priority low - 1 / medium - 3 / high - 9	1	1	1	1	1	1	1	1		
item	Weight / importance low - 1 / medium - 3 / high - 9	Customer Expectations	Design features	Internal Volume (Oz or ml)	Size (cubic feet / mm³)	Color	Type of Material	Shape	coating / Painting	Insulation	Lid	Weight Score	relative Weight Score
1	3	Big (fill a lot of cofee)		9	9			3				53	6%
2	3	fit in car support		3	9			9				53	6%
3	9	look like myself				9		9	9			243	25%
4	9	don't drop coffee into car (because of motion)						9			9	162	16%
5	1	warm hand					9	3		9		21	2%
6	9	don't burn hand					9	3		9		189	19%
7	9	Keep coffee warm						9		9	9	243	25%
		Weight / importance		36	54	81	171	228	81	171	162	984	100%
		Max Weight in the column		9	9	9	9	9	9	9	9	984	100%
		Relative Weight		4%	5%	8%	17%	23%	8%	17%	16%		
		Ranking		8	7	5	2	1	5	2	4		

It is almost evident that using this tool to develop a mug is like killing a fly using a cannon. Nevertheless, this example evidences how useful and powerful this tool can be to improve each aspect of your product, design or business.

Ok Marlon. This looks like too theoretical to me. How can I try another hands-on approach?

Certainly, the next method that I will show you is the tool that you should use to collect and evaluate data, mainly for the last methods.

5.5   Blind Experience method

This method is an amazing empirical tool which helps you to improve the quality of your products/services in quite few interactions.

Have you ever heard about Placebo effect?

In medical and pharmacological developments, they test the effects of drugs in humans. Nevertheless, people are complex and difficult to measure. Because of that, part of drugs pills of trial are placebos . They look like the actual pills, but they are not (can be sugar, flour, et cetera). The only ones who know which pills were placebo are the researchers.

In the blind experience method, the placebo effect is the driver motor of method.

This method consist in 4 steps:

Step 1

Prepare 3 products/ objects where each one has a different features to be evaluated.

Do you Remember the customer driven service? That is the time that you can apply a lot.

It is important to note that the only thing different among the objects must be the feature.

Prepare 2 objects with **NO FEATURE.**

Exposes only 3 of products/object in a small group of clients (3 to 5 people)

Try hard to select all from the same type of customer. Give preference to ordinary customers.

Check which one they like the most.

Replace one of products and repeat step 3 again until of parts have been compared.

It might finish in 5 to 7 interactions.

By the end, you will have the score of each feature that you are evaluating so that you can rank and improve your techniques.

"Creativity is nothing but the way to solve new problems."

Diana Santos

6 How to optimize your work and environment

Considering that you have already learn about creativity methods, Concept selection tools and Development approaches, I will show you some tools and methods that will help you to optimize your productivity and creativity.

This chapter was divided in 2 parts which describe: **methods to change and optimize your environment;** and **valuable tools to help you to maximize your productivity and management.**

6.1 Environment Changes

As explained in previous chapters, the environment affects our focus, in addition to divergent thinking and convergent thinking.

For that reason several companies invest a significant amount of money in architecture that induce creativity and focus.

The main goal of this chapter is to expose you a couple techniques that you can implement in your daily basis or even in your company.

Those techniques will also help you to implement creativity tools and implement incremental and disruptive innovation.

6.1.1   Removing noises

When we start talking about noises, we imagine sounds and acoustic noises in the environment. In fact, background noise affects our focus and creativity, as we have already explained in previous chapters.

However, I will show you now that our life and routine tasks are affected by different noises.

Those noises can be anything that make you move away from your goals.

For example, imagine that you are studying a very important and difficult subject. You know that this matter is extremely important and it is also aligned with your goals.

Then you decided to study at your grandmothers' home (or in someplace where the owner cooks amazingly).

After the 10 first minutes of study, you feel a delicious smell of chocolate cake that you grandmother put in the oven.

Then, 30 minutes later, the chocolate cake smell intensifies because of the coffee smell has been prepared for the afternoon tea time.

As you realized, this environment has driven you away from your task and goals, even though it was delicious and makes you instantaneously happy.

In daily basis, several tasks and events generate noises that drive you away from your goals. Such as sounds, games, social media, news , or any other thing that is not aligned with your goals.

As a consequence, it implies you need to change your habits from the point that several negative habits stop jeopardize your work.

So, the first thing that you need to know is that you have to **remove** these **noises** and **include gold tasks** (tasks that are aligned with your goals).

The 10 seconds rule

Most of human beings have the procrastination flowing into their veins. It means that we instinctively try to void or postpone any task that is aligned with our animal instincts.

Therefore, when someone thinks about doing some task, the first moments until the task begin are highlighted by the mind battle. Part of our mind try to justify and convince ourselves not to engage in other task that is not as comfortable as the current state that we already is. The logical part of our brain try argue us to engage in this new task.

The point in this situation is the fact that the part of our mind that defends we to stay in the comfortable zone wins in most of times.

Longer you take to start a new task harder it gets you to start it.

For that reason, the **10 seconds rule** indicates that any task that takes **less than 10 seconds** to start has **high probabilities** to be engaged.

Any task that takes **more than 10 seconds** to start has **low probabilities** to be engaged.

Thus, **define tasks** that are **important** and you want to include into your routine and **make it easier to start**.

For example, I always wanted to improve my musical skills and justified that I had no time to practice.

Following the 10 seconds rule, I put my guitar in the middle of our lobby room in order to have free and easy access to my guitar in less than 10 seconds.

As a consequence, I start practicing very short periods of guitar playing between work tasks.

It is important to note that Playing guitar and increase music skill was part of my goals. Otherwise, it would be considered a noise.

Another example can be applied with regards to games and social media. After identifying that I spend a really amount of time in games and social media, I decided to apply the 10 seconds rule to reduce or remove these noises from my daily routine.

In order to implement it, I put my console in the original box and stored it in the deeper drawer of my closet. It takes 1,5 minutes to take the box and connect in the TV.

As a consequence, I reduced my game time in 90%, increasing my available time for other things more aligned with my goals.

Defining Priorities

Another thing that most of human beings do is to create and accumulate extra tasks into the daily journey.

In most of cases, the extra tasks are not aligned with our goals, even though we think they were important at the moment. In addition, people also confuse productivity with being busy.

Therefore, our limbic system lead us to feel the achievement of meanless tasks.

Thus, I will show you how to use your cognition and logic to "trick" your limbic system and be aligned with your goals.

First thing is to create priorities and daily goals for your tasks and daily routines.

You can start low profile and organize your day using **80/20 Rule**. In this case, 80% of all your daily tasks correspond to 20% of your actual achievement (aligned with your goals). So, you need to **increase your focus and your energy on these 20%**.

Use **Priority Box (described in next section)** to establish what is REALLY important for you and remove noise tasks that we invent to sabotage ourselves.

After remove the noise tasks, apply the **1-3-5 method (described in next section)** to organize your routine. In this method you will chose 1 big thing (important and time consuming), 3 medium thing (medium importance or medium time consuming) and 5 small things (low importance and fast to do).

This method will bring you the benefits of accomplishment and force your body to release dopamine and increase your happiness.

In addition, it will make you spend more time in the 20% most important task of yours.

6.1.2   Motivate Innovation and creativity

Now that you learn a little bit about prioritizing, I will show you a couple techniques to help you to motivate Innovation and creativity of your team, your company and even yourself.

Each one has a different motivation which is the fuel that feed the life engine. Nevertheless, several studies reveal that our motivation depends on our primitive needs .

Maslow (1954) indicates a "hierarchy of needs" which describes our basic needs until the most sophisticated needs.

Figure 59

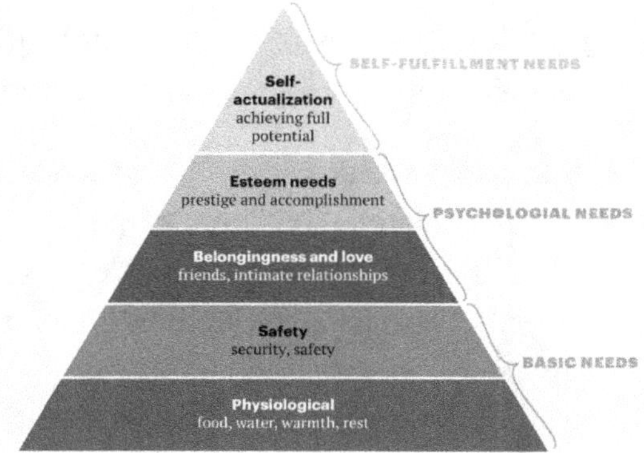

Therefore, it is possible to establish that our motivation is dynamic and depends on the personal situation.

For example, Douglas Mcgregor (1960) indicated a comparison between 2 contrasting stereotypes: X and Y.

The X type avoids responsibilities, being conscientious and people-oriented. As a consequence, they need to be controlled and defined task.

On the other hand, the Y type enjoys working (usually workaholic), seek responsibility and are task-oriented. In contrast with X type, they need space to develop imagination.

As you must have realized, both of the people type are different and totally different to motivate.

Therefore, how to find motivation?

Herberg (1968) indicated contrasting motivation fuels in 2 categories: Motivators and Hygiene Factors.

1. **'Motivators'** - factors giving rise to satisfaction
   a. Related to Content of Work
   b. Promote Satisfaction
   c. More indicated to new generations
2. **'Hygiene factors'** - factors giving rise to dissatisfaction
   a. Related to context/environment of work
   b. Only prevent Dissatisfaction
   c. Widely applied in old school companies

It is possible to indicate that motivators are highly connected to the top of Maslow pyramid, while hygiene factors are linked to basic needs of Maslow pyramid.

The table bellow presents examples of motivators and hygiene factors in order you to better understand the situation of your team and act on those aspects.

Motivators	Hygienes
Achivement	Company policy and recognition
Recognition	Supervision – technical aspects
Work itself	Salary

Responsibility	Interpersonal relations – supervision
Advancement	Working conditions

On the other hand, each one has a part of brain which is more required . And it also reflect on the motivation and the way that people behave and see the future.

One way to understand this is the **Hermann Brain Dominance Instrument (HBDI).**

In this method, the brain is divided in 4 quadrants where the dominance of each part of brain will lead to the sort of thinking of each one.

Figure 60

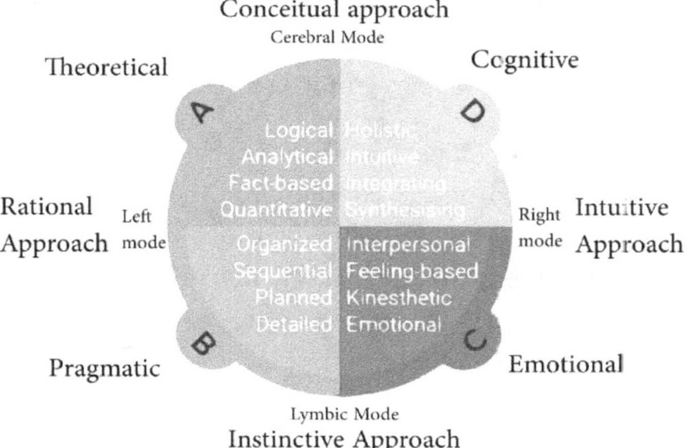

A. Analytical thinking are driven by logical, factual, critical, technical, quantitative thinking. They are more comfortable working with activities that involve: collecting data, analysis, understanding how things work, judging ideas based on facts, criteria and logical reasoning.

B. Sequential thinking are driven by safekeeping, structured, organized, complexity or detailed, planned. They are more comfortable working with activities that involve: following directions, detail-oriented work, step-by-step problem solving, organization, implementation.

C. Interpersonal thinking are driven by kinesthetic, emotional, spiritual, sensory, feeling. They are more comfortable working with activities that involve: listening to and expressing ideas, looking for personal meaning, sensory input, group interaction.

D. Imaginative thinking are driven by visual, holistic, intuitive, innovative, conceptual. They are more comfortable working with activities that involve: looking at the big picture, taking initiative, challenging assumptions, visuals, metaphoric thinking, creative problem solving, long-term thinking.

Aligning with the knowledge that you acquired about creativity, it is possible to understand that the thinking style diversity will generate more creative team. Therefore, creating and managing teams that contain a good distribution of thinking styles will help you to overcome struggles, solve problems and develop opportunities.

Figure 61

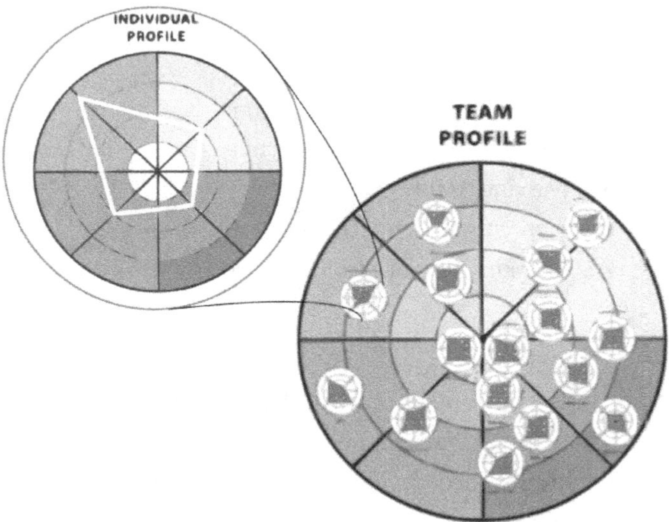

Removing Barriers to Creativity and Innovation

As part of our daily job to increase motivation and removing noises, several researchers identified barriers that jeopardize self-esteem and destroy motivation aspects.

I will list the 7 most important obstacles that you have to remove from your life, company or team in order to improve quality, create stimulus to innovate and being creative:

1. Negativity
2. Fear of failure
3. Lack of quality thinking time
4. Over-conformance with rules and regulations
5. Making assumptions
6. Applying too much logic
7. Thinking you are not creative

In order to fight against those barriers, I will present a couple of tricks that will help you. Nevertheless, plenty of techniques are available and there is no simple answer for this situation. You will have to test by try and fail method until find one that suits you.

Negativity generates plenty of damage, it is known that **1 negative** thought correspond to **3 to 7 positive** thoughts.

Therefore, before saying any negative idea or criticizing idea, make a really strong effort to say **at least 3 positive comments** about one idea.

Fear of Failure

Failure is one natural thing that people need to learn how to handle in order to grow and self improve.

An environment that pressure people not to failure will block people to try new things, experiment different approaches and being creative.

It is important to note that failing is not as important as how to solve the problems and consequence caused by failures.

Create an environment that don't punish people for being different in order to build inventors and generative partners.

Lack of quality thinking time

Most of us has already heard or said that has NO time to implement ideas or think different.

In fact, time is a concept that is almost invariable in the universe and we can only manage how to use it. I will recommend 2 approaches that will improve productivity and creativity.

The first idea came from a research performed in Europe. This research indicated that the most creative researches generated there prime idea during coffee time. Why?

Simple. When you are distracted from the current stressful task, your mind run away to rest. The process that it happens generates cross connections of ideas and generates new things. This is why we dream when we sleep and because of that several strange things happen during dreams, isn't it?

Take a quality time to do NOTHING related to work in order o activate this cognition.

The second thing is to organize your time. Use different approaches in order to guarantee your free thoughts time during the day. It can be done all in once or in small periods during the day.

As a consequence, you will train your brain to produce more ideas and as a consequence, you will increase thinking agility.

Over-conformance with rules and regulations

It is important to note that rules and regulations are important and organize our society.

But on the other hand, we can say that the truth about the universe is temporary and depends on the community acceptance, perspectives and needs.

Therefore, questioning standards, rules and regulations will help you to update needs and demands, making you think outside the box.

In this context the box are the rules and regulations.

Take a look in the previous chapter "think outside the box" the discover that most of techniques will help you to confront rules and pre-existent concepts in order to create new things.

Thinking you are not creative

As you have already discovered in this book, creativity is not only thing that you born with. It is a skill that you develop and cultivate.

Therefore, take a step further and engage yourself in creativity tools and techniques in order to get benefits to your personal and professional life.

" Almost always, the creative dedicated minority has made the world better."

Martin Luther King

6.2.1   Trello

Description: Trello is a web system that allow you to create to do lists in a Kanban Board format. In this system, theme boards, lists and cards in order to organize your tasks.

Figure 62

The most basic organization of Trello Kanban boards consist on moving the cards from the "to do" list through "doing" list until the "done" list. Therefore, everyone in the team board can visually see the status of each task of sprint.

Lists:

- To do

- Doing
- Done

Cards:

- Tasks
- Subprojects
- To do lists
- Goals
- Deliveries
- Et cetera

Applications:

Stock Control	Design Thinking	Design Sprint
Brain Storming	Morphological Chart	Creativity tools
Concept Selection	Pomodoro method	Project Management
To do List	Check list	Cost Control
Production control	Process control	Book Organization

Suitable for groups from **1 to 7 people.**

6.2.2 Gantt Project

Description: Gantt Project is an open-source software that helps you to organize and manage project, tasks and production. It generates Gantt diagram, project schedule, resource accountability in addition to having Pert (Program Evaluation Review Technique) and CPM (Critical Path Method). As Result, It is an wonderful alternative for MS Project and Primavera.

Figure 63

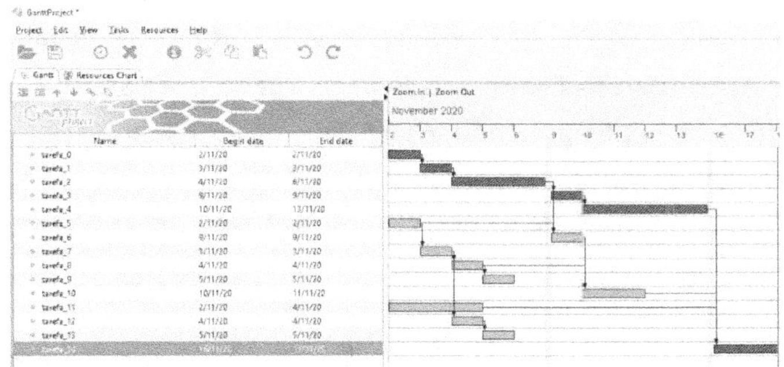

Applications:

Production Control	Design Thinking	Design Sprint
Brain Storming	Morphological Chart	Product Development
Concept Selection	Task Prioritization	Project Management
Process control	Check list	Cost Control

Suitable for groups from **1 to 50 people**.

6.2.3   Team Gantt and Wrinkle

Description: Team Gantt and Wrikle are web Based system that helps you to organize and manage project, tasks and production with a **simultaneous link with Trello**. It generates Gantt diagram while creates and manages cards and list in Trello. As other classical project management softwares, it also project schedule, resource accountability in addition to having Pert (Program Evaluation Review Technique) and CPM (Critical Path Method). On the other hand, those systems also support several metrics and indicators, such as Burn Down, Burn Up, Sprint rate, Earn Points, among others.

As Result, It is an wonderful alternative for MS Project and Primavera.

Figure 64

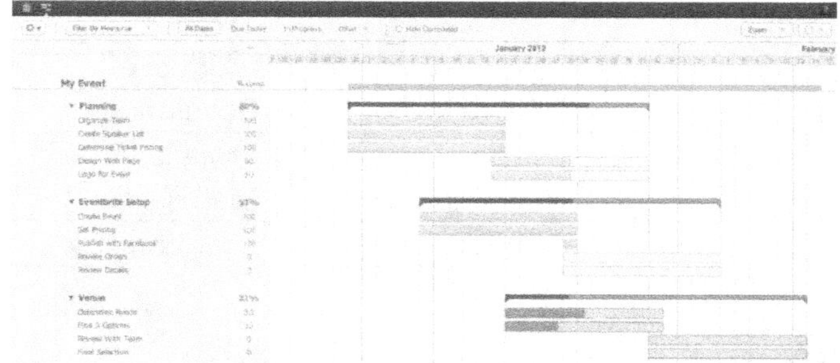

Applications:

Production Control	Design Thinking	Design Sprint
Brain Storming	Morphological Chart	Product Development
Concept Selection	Task Prioritization	Project Management
Process control	Check list	Cost Control

Suitable for groups from **1 to 50 people**

6.2.4   Pomodoro

Description: Pomodoro is a technique that allow you to increase focus and optimize your time. It consists in short periods of fully focused work (no disruption is allowed) followed by 5 minutes of break.

Figure 65

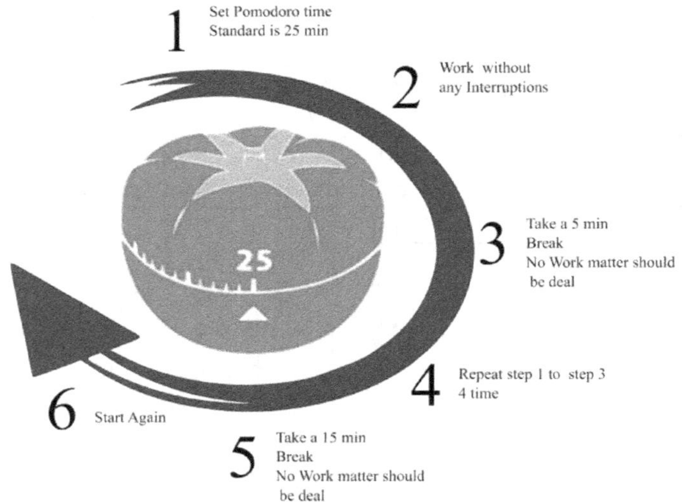

Applications:

Productivity	Creativity Sessions	Structured Arguing
Negotiation		

Suitable for groups from **1 to 3 people** simultaneously.

6.2.5   Priority box

Description: Priority Box is an amazing tool that helps you to prioritize what is REALLY important for you. In other words, it help you to see and remove noises and tasks that do not contribute to your goals.

The Priority BOX
(Eisenhower Matrix)

	Low Ungency	High Ungency
High Importance	Do Next (or Schedule)	Do First (or As Soon As Possible)
Low Importance	DON'T DO	Do Late (or Delegate)

How Important is this Taks/Project?

How Urgent is this Taks/Project?

The general idea is kind of simple. Each task or project that you need to do will be classified as in 2 dimension: Importance and Urgency.

You classify the tasks by answering:

How Important is this task?

- Extremely important (High importance)
- Very important (High Importance)
- Important (low Importance)
- Not important (low Importance)

How Urgent is this task?

- Extremely Urgent (High importance)
- Very Urgent (High Importance)

- Necessary (low Importance)
- Not urgent (low Importance)

Then, according the 2 dimension classification, each task will be put in one of the 4 quadrants of the priority box. It makes that you prioritize and act on the task according to:

Action: **Do it NOW**

- **HIGH** importance
- **HIGH** Urgency

Action: **Do it NEXT**

- **High** importance
- **LOW** Urgency

Action: **Do it LATE**

- **LOW** importance
- **High** Urgency

Action: **DON'T DO IT**

- **LOW** importance
- **LOW** Urgency

Applications:

Design Sprint	Project Management	Design Thinking
Personal	Habit Changing	Creativity

management		Sessions
Innovation		
Strategy		

Suitable for groups from **1 to 7 people**.

6.2.6   1-3-5 Method

Description: 1-3-5 method is an empirical method or rule that helps your brain to see your productiveness. As presented before in this book, our brain confuses being busy and being productive, as a biochemical response obtained by finishing and achieving goals.

Figure 67

1 Big Thing
Very important things that demand large amount of time to finish

3 Medium Things
Important tasks that demand medium amount of time to finish

5 Little Things
Tasks (usually not super important) that are fast to finish

In order to trick our brain, the 1-3-5 method defines, as a basic rule, that your daily routine need to be composed by only 9 tasks.

1 very important task, which is highly aligned with your goals. In general, these tasks are time consuming and demands lot of time. In most of cases, those tasks might run during days or even month.

3 Important task, which are aligned with your goals but not as important as the very important task. In general, these tasks are not excessively time consuming but demands some time to complete. In most of cases, those tasks might 1 to 3 hours.

5 Quotidian tasks , which is necessary but not entirely aligned with your goals. In general, these tasks can be done fast and can be used distributed during your day. In most of cases, those tasks might take around 30 min to complete.

References

ADAMS, James . Conceptual Blockbusting . Reading, MA: Addison- Wesley, 1986.

ALTSHULLER, G. (H. Altov) . An(i Suddenly the Inventor Appeared, 1996.

ALTSHULLER, G.S . Creativity as an Exact Science. Luxemburgo:Gordon and Breach Publishers, 1984 .

AMABILE, Teresa M. Creativity ín Context . Boulder, CO: Westview Press, 1996.

ARIETI, Silvano. Creativity, the Magíc Synthesis. NEW York: Basic Books, Inc, 1976 .

BURNS, T., STALKER, G .M . The Management of Innovation. London: Tavistock, 1961.

BUZAN, Tony. Use Both Sides of Your Brain. NewYork : Dutton, 1983.

CAMERON, Julia. The Artist' s Way. Los Angeles: Jeremy P. Tarcher /Perigee, 1992.

CSIKSZENTMIHAL YI, Mihaly. Creativity. NewYork: HarperCollins, 1996 .

DEBONO, Edward. Seríous Creativity. NewYork : HarperCollins, 1993.

DEBONO, Edward . Six Thinking Hats . Toronto: Key Porter Books, Ltd., 1985.

FORD, Camcron M ., G TO IA, Dennis A. Creative Actio1 1 s in Orga1 1izalion s. Thousand Oaks, CA: Sage Publications , 1995 .

FRITZ, Rob e rt. The Pat/, of Least Resistance. NewYork: Ballantine Books, 1989 .

GARDNER, Howard. Creating Mi1 1d s. NewYork: Basic Books, Inc., 1993.

GARDNER, Howard. Lending Mind s. N ova York: Basic Books, Inc., 199 5 .

GLOVER, John A ., RONNING, R.R. , REYNOLD S, C. R. , (ed s .) Handbook of Creativity . NewYork: Plenum Press, 1989 .

GORDON, William J. , Synetictics. NewYork: Harper & Row, 1961.

G RON HAUG , K ., KAUFMANN, Geir (eds .) Innovations: A Cross- Disciplinary Perspective. Oslo: Norwegian University Press, 1988.

ISAKSEN, Scott G., MURDOCK, Mary C. , FIRESTIEN, Roger, TREFFINGER, Dona ld J., eds. Nurturing and Developing Creativity: The Emergence of a Discipline . Norwood, N J : Ablex, 1993 .

ISAKSEN, Scott G ., MURDOCK, Mary C. , FIRESTIEN, Roger, TREFFINGER, Donald J ., (e d s .)

Understanding and Recognizing Creativity: The
Emergence of a Discipline. Norwood, NJ :Ablex, 1993.

ISAKSEN, Scott, ed. Frontiers of Creativity Research:
Beyond the Basics. Buffalo, NewYork: Bearly
Limited , 1987.

KAO, John. Jamming: The Art and Discipline of
Business Creativity. NewYork : HarperCollins, 1996 .

KUCZMARSKI, Thom as D . Innovation. Chicago:
NTC Business Books, 1996 .

LEONARD-BARTON, Doroty . Well Springs of
Knowledge. Bo s ton: Harvard Business School
Press, 1995 .

MA TTIMORE, Bryan. 99% Inspiration . NewYork:
American Management Association, 1994.

MICHALKO, Michael. Thinker toys: A HandBook of
Business Creativity for the 90s. Berkeley,
CA: Ten Speed Press, 1991.

MILLER, William C. The Creative Edge. Reading, MA:
Addison-Wesley, 1987 .
MORGAN, Gareth. Creative Organization Theory .
Newbury P ark, CA: Sage Publications, 1989 .

MORGAN, Gareth. Images of Organization. 2 . ed.
Newbury Park, CA: Sage Publications, 1997.

MORGAN, Gareth . Imaginization: Toe Art of Creative
Management. Newbury Park, CA : Sage
Publications , 1997.

Nadler, Gerald, and Shozo Hibino. Breakthrough thinking. Prima Pub. & Communications, 1990.

OSBORN, Alex F. Applied imagination . 3 ed . Buffalo, NEW York: Creative Education Foundation Press, 1993 .

PARNES, Sidney J ., H . F. HARDING , e d . A Source Book for Creative Thinking. NewYork : Charles Scribner and Sons, 1962 .

PUGH, Stuart . Creating innovative Products Using Total Design . Reading , MA: Addison - Wesley ,1996.

RAY, Michael, M YE RS , Rochelle . Creativity in Business. NewYork : Doubleday, 1986.

Stein, Morris I. Stimulating creativity: Individual procedures. Academic Press, 2014.

STEIN, Morris I. Stimulating Creativity. Group Procedures. New York : Academic Press, 1975 . V . 2.

STERNBERG , Robert J., (e d .) The Nature of Creativity. Cambridge, MA: Cambridge University Press, 1988 .

Tanner, David. Total creativity in business & industry: road map to building a more innovative organization. Advanced Practical Thinking Training, 1997.

WEST , Michael A . , FA RR, James L., (eds.) Innovation and Creativity at Work. Chichester, Inglaterra: John Wiley & Sons. Ltd., 1990 .

WYCOFF J M d M . Your Personal Guide to Exploring
Creativity and Problem-Solving. New York: Berkley
Publishing Group, 1991.

WESCHLER, s. m. "Criatividade: descobrindo e
encorajando", campinas Psy, 1993

DUNCAN , William R. A Guide to the Project
management Body of Knowledge [s .1: s .n .] 1996

MARTIN , Paula , TATE, Karen. Project Management
Memory jogger™ . Methuen, MA : GOAL \QPC , 1997.

WYSOCKI , Robert W. , ROBERT BECK JR, CRANE,
David B. Effective Project Management. 1995 .

GOAL \ QPC e Joiner Associates . The Team Memory
Jogger TM_ Methuen, MA: GOAL \ QPC, 1995 .

Katzenbach, Jon R. e Douglas K. Smith. The Wisdom
of Team s. NewYork: HarperCollins, 1993.

Brassard , Michael. The Memory Jogger Plus +®.
Methuen, MA: GOAL \QPC, 1989 .

Brassard , Michael , Diane Ritter, et al. Coach 's Guide
to Memory Jogger™ II: The Easy-to-Use, Complete
Reference for Working with improvement and Planning
Tools in Teams. Methuen, MA: GOAL \ QPC, 1995 .

Brassard , Michael e Diane Ritter The Memory
Jogger™ II : Mehuen, MA: GOAL \QPC, 1994.

Clausing, Don . Total Quality Development: A Step-by-Step Guide to World-Class Concurrent Engineering . American Society of Mechanical Egineers. 1994.

Deming, W . Edwards. Out of the Crisis . Cambridge, MA: MIT Center for Advanced Engineering Study, 1986 .

Deming, W. Edwards . The New Economics: For lndustry, Government, Education . Cambridge, MA: MIT Center for Advanced Engineering Study, 1993 .

King, Bob . Better Designs in Half the Time: Implementing Quality Function Deployment in America. Methuen, MA: GOAL \ QPC, 1989.
A. Run co & Robert S. Albert (ed s.), Theories of Creativity, Newbury Park, CA: Sage Publications, 1990, 61-91.

Amabile, Teresa M. e Elisabe th Tighe . "Questions of Creativity ." Em John Brockman (ed .), Creativity. NewYork: Simon & Shuster, 1993, 7-27.

Damanpour, Fariborz. " Organizational Innovation: A Meta-Analysis of Effects of Determinants and Moderators. " Academy of Management Journal 34 555-590.

Gardner, Howard. " Creative Lives and Creative Works : A Syntetic Scientific Approach." In Robert Sternberg (ed.), The Nature of Creativity, 1988. Cambridge, MA: Cambridge University Press , (pp. 298-321).

Guilford, J.P. "Creativity: A Quarter Century of Progress ." in I.A. Taylor & J.W. Getzels (eds .), Perspectives in Creativity, 1975 . Chicago: Aldine Publishing Company (pp. 37-59).

Harrington , Donald M . " The Ecology o f Human Creativity: A Psychological Perspective." In Mark A. Runco & Robert S. Albert (e d s.), Theories of Creativity. Newbury Park, CA : Sage Publications, 1990, 143 -1 69.

Isaksen , Scott G , Gerard J. Pucci o, e Donald J. Treffinger. "An Eco logical Approach to Creativity Research: Profiling for Creative Problem Solving." The Journal of Creative Behavior 27: 149-170.

Kanter", Rosabeth M . "When a Thous and Flowers Bloom: Structural, Collective, and Social Conditions for Innovation in Organization." ln Barry M . Staw & Larry L. Curnmings (eds.), Research in Organizational Behavior, 10 (1988) : 169-211.

Puccio, Gerard J. "An Overview of Creativity Assessment." The Assessmen t of Creativity: An Occasional Paper from the Creativity Based Information Resources Project, 1994, 5-20 .

Quinn, Jam es. B. "Managing Innovation: Controlled Chaos." Harvard Business Review: 73-85.

Tushman, Michael e David Nadler. "Organizing for Innovation ." California Management Review 74-92 .

Woodman, Richard W., John E. Sawyer e Ricky W
.Griffin. "Toward a Theory of Organizational Creativity
." Academy of Management Review 18 293-321.

www.ingramcontent.com/pod-product-compliance
Lightning Source LLC
Chambersburg PA
CBHW061332250726
48657CB00004B/1129